6 - 21 - 73

POLICE UNIONS

POLICE

UNIONS

By

ALLEN Z. GAMMAGE, Ph.D.

*Professor of Police Science and
Administration
Sacramento State College
Sacramento, California*

and

STANLEY L. SACHS, M.A.

*Management Research Consultant
Sacramento, California*

CHARLES C THOMAS · PUBLISHER
Springfield · Illinois · U.S.A.

Published and Distributed Throughout the World by
CHARLES C THOMAS • PUBLISHER
BANNERSTONE HOUSE
301-327 East Lawrence Avenue, Springfield, Illinois, U.S.A.
NATCHEZ PLANTATION HOUSE
735 North Atlantic Boulevard, Fort Lauderdale, Florida, U.S.A.

© *1972, by* CHARLES C THOMAS • PUBLISHER

ISBN 0-398-02467-7

Library of Congress Catalog Card Number: 70-190323

With **THOMAS BOOKS** *careful attention is given to all details of*
manufacturing and design. It is the Publisher's desire to present books
that are satisfactory as to their physical qualities and artistic possibilities
and appropriate for their particular use. THOMAS BOOKS *will be true*
to those laws of quality that assure a good name and good will.

Printed in the United States of America
HH-11

PREFACE

This book is a limited evaluation of the theory and practice of unionization of police agencies in the United States. Its writers characterize our presentation as *limited* since we were largely confined to the utilization of available pertinent literature and the use of correspondence techniques in an effort to acquire new data.

In accomplishing the research phase of the project, a literature search was made by subject title and breakdown, using the California State Library, Sacramento; Sacramento State College Library; Sacramento City Library, Main Branch; Sacramento County Library, Carmichael Branch; Aerojet Liquid Rocket Company Technical Information Center, and California Peace Officers' Standards and Training Reference Room, Sacramento.

Discussions were held with employees in various police agencies located in the Greater Sacramento Area, as well as state and federal law enforcement personnel.

Letters of inquiry were sent to labor and public law enforcement officials in each of the fifty states, as well as to officers of national organizations. Additional letters of inquiry were mailed to private individuals who are active or associated with any aspect of police unionization when these were known.

Since the cities of Vallejo and Antioch, California were the scenes of police strikes in 1969 and 1970, respectively, these were visited and strike information accumulated.

Primary sources for statistical information regarding the national scene and individual states were two booklets published by the International Association of Chiefs of Police in 1944 and 1958 along with a more recent publication, *The Police Labor Movement* by John H. Burpo (Charles C Thomas, Publisher, 1971). Insights into the early "police strikes" largely stems from a single source, a 1940 book, *One Thousand Strikes of Government Employees* (Columbia University Press).

Additionally, a number of other books are available (and were used) which deal with the general evolution of the labor movement in the United States. However, it appears that concern with police unions is very brief and only passing in almost all instances. Even the U. S. Department of Labor's bibliography concerning police unions largely is confined to references in articles in periodicals, which proved to be the only other sources of published data.

Apparently, some additional and sporadic efforts have been exerted to document the police union movement by individuals in various parts of the country. However, even when a "lead" to these works was uncovered, they were not readily available through normal library sources. Also, police unionization articles and studies written since 1958 are largely philosophical discourses regarding the "right" of public employees to unionize or to strike, or they deal with the problem on a highly limited basis, confining their presentations to specific geographical areas.

Moreover, a significant problem was encountered throughout the research in that individuals directly participating in the police union movement showed an extreme reluctance to openly discuss the problems associated with it or even to give its status. When personal interviews were held with a number of police employees, their opinions are subsequently reflected in our work in an anonymous fashion (at their request). In most instances written inquiries were ignored, side-stepped, or responses were either "off the record" or presented in mere generalities. Along these lines, it is interesting to note that even the International Association of Chiefs of Police (1958) experienced difficulty in obtaining answers to its questionnaires—only twenty-six states responded. In these writers' own experiences, one California newspaper even denied that a "police strike" had occurred in the community, despite the fact that the incident had been reported by the wire services.

In any event, these writers believe that the book is comprehensive, will assist in filling a "literary gap" and prove helpful to police administrators, public administrators, public officials, students of personnel management, and working police personnel in understanding the extent and ramifications of the police union movement—one of the most significant of police personnel management problems today.

After a brief introduction, the book presents a capsuled, historical account of the evolution of the total union movement in the United States, the development of public employee and police unions from the late 1800's to the present time, recent developments on the California scene, and a digest of known police union/association organizational activities (along with labor legislation).

Chapter VII presents pre-World War II views on police union membership, collective bargaining, and strikes; current arguments regarding each of these, and explains the conditions now working toward possible complete, future unionization of the police.

The final chapter presents the historical significance of the developments that have occurred and offers the writers' conclusions and recommendations as they relate to the solution of a problem of utmost importance to the police and our society as a whole.

ALLEN Z. GAMMAGE
STANLEY L. SACHS

CONTENTS

POLICE UNIONS

Chapter I

INTRODUCTION

The history of the union movement in the United States is replete with abortive attempts to enlist police employees into trade unions as well as highly unsatisfactory results in instances where such unionization has succeeded. Periodically, we have also experienced renewed efforts to organize United States policemen into formal labor unions of their own. Frequently, the newspapers report on "blue power" stirrings of discontent among the rank and file members of police unionization. Concurrently, organized labor, as well as independent groups, appear poised —ready to take full advantage of local problems to accomplish this unionization.

Although classic tradition says that police unions are incompatible with the public service, these writers find little available empirical evidence to either substantiate or refute this contention. Yet, we find a growing militancy on the part of law enforcement personnel to assert their "working rights" by applying some of the more traditional labor techniques: mass sick leaves, slowdowns, sick-ins, sick-outs, and strikes. When these incidents do occur, they largely leave the community both shocked and unprepared to cope with them, particularly at first exposure. Often the community starts out almost ostrich-like—burying its head in the sand, pretending that a police labor problem does not even exist. Once the "disagreement" moves into the work stoppage or secondary boycott stage, community leaders appear to be galvanized into emotional reaction. They seek to reassure the community, while panicking themselves; heroic deeds of manning the deserted police posts by the unqualified and unequipped becomes the order of the day, and the tocsin is sounded for state or even National Guard assistance.

Unlike the Boston police strike of 1919, when some 1,500

3

striking policemen were permanently discharged from the force, today's striking policemen who asserts his "blue power" usually obtains a collective bargaining agreement, increased wages, amnesty, and an arrangement for no loss in wages during the period he was on strike. Community officials then behave as though the act had never occurred, rather than face future possibilities realistically. Therefore, without derogating the issues which lead policemen to such drastic actions, the question must be raised as to what is actually in the best interests of the public: that which we have previously witnessed—more formalized dealings with police unions and police associations or compulsory arbitration of grievances? Anything but a cursory examination of the pressing question is beyond the scope of this study; however, the question itself is valid and substantiates the fact that American communities, for the most part, are not equipped to cope with the problem of police unionization when it appears in any one of its current guises.

Conversely, sufficient empirical evidence is available to show that policemen in many parts of the country are being swept into labor-organized union activities or independent associations that act as sub rosa police unions. The failure of wages to keep pace with the rising cost of living is a chief cause for this activity. Other considerations include poor working conditions, loss of status and prestige, and the increased difficulty of police tasks attributed to social phenomena and liberal politics.

Clinging to the 1919 doctrines of Calvin Coolidge, as enunciated in connection with the Boston police strike, local governments have not developed an empirical basis for an enlightened approach to their own labor relations with public safety employees. They also show remarkable opposition to the concepts of compulsory arbitration, apparently on an emotional rather than a factual basis. Thus, the major point emerging from this research is the vital need for a formally endowed program to accomplish an in-dept study of the contemporary police union movement in the United States. The results from such a study should be combined into a source book and broadly dispersed to provide an objective basis for local government judgements and actions in connection with their labor relations policies for public safety employees. The greatest potential for successful negotiations of this type rests with their being accomplished before employees strike rather than during or after such drastic action.

Chapter II

EVOLUTION OF THE UNION MOVEMENT
IN THE UNITED STATES

The Industrial Revolution appeared almost simultaneously with the intellectual, scientific, and political revolutions of the seventeenth and eighteenth centuries. Most simplistically, it consisted of developing machines, linking power to these machines, and subsequently establishing factories wherein a large number of people were employed. These combinations resulted in enormous increases in the productive power of man, accompanied by minute subdivisions of labor, unsavory factory conditions, and extensive child labor abuse.

Economically, the Industrial Revolution resulted in major increases in output as well as great accumulations of goods and capital. This accelerated business and commerce significantly improved the social and economic status of owners and entrepreneurs. However, the average employee faired very poorly as to his working conditions, as well as in his purchasing power. "Labor was considered a commodity to be bought and sold, and the prevailing political philosophy of 'laissez faire' resulted in little action by governments to protect or improve the lot of the workers."[1]

It was from this foundation of worker exploitation and fear that the concepts of free collective bargaining emerged. Until the mid-1850's, little legal protection for workers existed. Any attempt at collective bargaining was punishable as an act of criminal conspiracy. Not until the *Commonwealth v. Hunt* decision of 1842 were workers allowed to organize or bargain collectively for ameliorated conditions.

Gradually, the expansion of education and the voting franchise to all citizens brought political strength to the workers, who

[1]Wendell French: *The Personnel Management Process: Human Resources Administration.* Boston, Houghton Mifflin Company, 1964, p. 11.

were able to gain the passage of certain protective legislation. The earliest form of these laws concerned hours of employment for women and children. These were followed by legislation covering hours of work for males, health and safety standards, and, finally, the right to bargain collectively with employers.

First concentrated upon the private sector, the concept of unionization spread through the ranks of public employees, starting early in this century. Largely abortive, particularly as they pertain to police organizations, these early attempts did lay the foundation for current activities which are becoming increasingly commonplace on the American scene. Therefore, some detailed historical treatment of the labor movement in the United States is essential if a realistic understanding of the existing trend in police agency unionization is to be achieved.

At the outset in examining unionism in the United States, several basic concepts can be considered as general principles concerning union growth in this country.[2]

First, the trade union is one of the oldest economic institutions in the United States. Actually, it predates our business corporation by a number of years. Additionally, the earliest unions are strikingly similar in their broad objectives to those existing today. The purposes for which workers join trade unions and the arguments advanced for and against union organizations have changed little since 1800.

Secondly, the trend in union membership has been steadily upward; no foreseeable change in this trend seems apparent. Actually, it now appears that this membership will continue to expand until almost all eligible public and private workers are members of the union.

Thirdly, the growth in union membership has been accomplished by a continuous penetration of unionism into new industries, occupations, and geographical areas. Unionism has spread from the skilled workers to the semiskilled and unskilled. Finally, it has reached the white-collar worker and into the ranks of public employees. Geographically, the spread has been from the large cities to the smaller municipalities and towns.

[2]Lloyd G. Reynolds: *Labor Economics and Labor Relations,* 2nd ed. New York. Prentice-Hall, 1954. pp. 40-41.

Fourthly, one notes a steady evolution of organizational structure. The first form of organization was the local union of workers in a specific trade or industry. This was followed by the development of federations which included all local unions in a particular city, then by national trade unions comprising all locals in an existing trade or industry throughout the country, and finally by federations of these national unions (i.e. AFL or CIO). Out of this development, the national trade union has emerged as the key organizational unit, more important than the local unions of which it is composed or the national federation to which it belongs.

Finally, unions organized on an industrial basis appear to dominate the national scene when compared with those organized on a craft basis.

EARLY ORGANIZED ACTIVITY

The earliest record of a labor disturbance in this country appears to have occurred in 1636 when a group of fishermen were reported to have fallen into "a mutany" when their wages were withheld.[3] Some forty years later, the licensed cartmen of New York, ordered to remove dirt from the streets for threepence a load, not only protested this low rate of pay, but "combined to refuse full compliance."[4] Other comparable incidents were occasionally reported in the colonial press during the eighteenth century. However, what was perhaps the first really authentic strike against employers occurred in 1768 with a "turn-out" of journeymen tailors in New York.[5] Approximately 20 workers struck, because of a reduction in wages, and publicly advertised that, in defiance of the master, they would take private work. They stated further that they would be on call at the Sign of the Fox and Hound; their notice in the paper read, "at the rate of three shillings and six pence per day, with diet."

Historians generally agree that the American labor organizations had their beginnings in the late eighteenth century before

---

[3]Foster R. Dulles: *Labor in America*. New York, Thomas Y. Crowell Company, 1966, pp. 20-21.
[4]*Ibid.*
[5]*Ibid.*

the emergence of the factory. However, these were combinations of businessmen and the self-employed in trade associations, which sought to affect prices or favorably alter the terms of sale. A union of wage earners differs from these associations in that it seeks to affect the terms of the wage bargain and to change the conditions under which its members are employed.

The first to organize was the skilled artisan: the printer, shoemaker, and building tradesman.[6] Like their successors, the early trade unions mainly were concerned with holding wage levels in order that they could maintain their standard of living as skilled workers. These were proud craftsmen who believed that their organizations excluded inferior men.[7]

The first union, established in 1792, was a society of Philadelphia shoemakers. It lasted one year, and even its name now is unknown.[8] In 1794, the Federal Society of Cordwainers was established in Philadelphia and became the first permanent union, remaining active until 1806, during which time it conducted a number of strikes. By the turn of the century, unions of shoemakers, carpenters, and printers were founded in Baltimore, Philadelphia, Boston, New York, and several other cities.

In 1799, the Franklin Typographical Society of Journeymen Printers of New York was formed. This society formulated the first complete wage scale ever adopted by the printers of New York City and went on strike to enforce it.[9] Early printers' unions displayed the same general attitudes as the shoemakers' journeymen organizations; they were primarily concerned with wages and working conditions.

From 1800 to 1810, those trades represented by labor organizations attempted to force increases in wages through strikes. Many of these labor groups had started as benevolent organizations and later changed their objectives. In 1804, the journeymen

---

[6]Philip Taft: *Organized Labor in American History.* New York, Harper & Row, 1964, p. 4.

[7]John R. Commons and associates (Eds.): *A Documentary History of American Industrial Society.* Cleveland, Arthur H. Clark Co., 1910, II, pp. 104-105.

[8]*Ibid.*

[9]Ethelbert Stewart: A documentary history of early organizations of printers. *Bulletin of the Department of Labor,* November 1905, p. 863.

tailors of Baltimore requested a wage increase and struck to enforce the demand. The next year, Philadelphia cordwainers
struck for higher wages, and this strike led to their indictment
for conspiracy to raise wages. A second strike by the Baltimore
tailors was called in 1808; the demand was again for higher wages.
Dissatisfaction spread to New York, where the well-organized shoemakers struck against a shop which refused to pay the union rate.
When the struck employer transferred his work to other shops,
a general strike of shoemakers was called in New York City. A
strike of shoemakers in Albany, New York, in 1810, for wage
increases also was reported.[10]

All of these early unions engaged in collective bargaining.
At the outset, union representatives visited each master separately,
with the price or wage lists that had been accepted at the meeting
of the union journeymen. This practice evolved into group bargaining. The first recorded collective bargaining was the negotiations between the Philadelphia cordwainers and their employers
in 1799. It followed a lockout after the workers refused to accept
a wage cut. A committee of workers called on the employers
who compromised the differences through a group of their own
representatives. However, the first clear-cut instance of collective
bargaining initiated by employees occurred in 1809 when the
New York Journeymen Printers formulated a price list and presented it to their employers. These employers met, considered
the proposals, and appointed a committee to negotiate with the
journeymen. Committees from both groups met several times
and negotiated a compromise.[11]

Strike benefits also received considerable attention from the
very outset of the labor movement. The Philadelphia printers
pledged themselves, in 1786, to support all journeymen forced
out of work due to their refusal to accept a wage cut. Money was
given to those workers and their families. This practice of financing striking workers was copied from the employers who
financed individual masters who were in difficulty. In 1805, the
New York shoemakers established a permanent defense fund.

---

[10]John R Commons, *et al, op. cit.,* III, pp. 62-63.
[11]*Ibid.,* I, p. 12.

Some of the early unions also paid sick and death benefits, depending upon the amount of surplus money the union had.[12]

The "closed shop" concept also was espoused right from the outset of the union movement. Early unions demanded that unorganized men be excluded from employment. Control over the supply of labor was characteristic of many early organizations. This is a charge that appears in almost all of the subsequent labor conspiracy trials.[13]

Conversely, early trade unions were highly unstable. Opposition from employers and government, as well as the loss of interest among members, frequently were fatal to the more fragile organizations. Another characteristic of these early unions was their inability to withstand business depression. They sprang up and flourished in the good years, but almost all of them disappeared during the depression years. It also appears that the growth of unionism has always followed the swings of the business cycle, particularly in the earlier years. The principal periods of growth and decline can be briefly summarized as follows:[14]

1. *1800-1815, Prosperity:* Shoemakers and printers organized local unions in a number of cities. Carpenters organized in a few places.
2. *1817-1821, Depression:* All of the shoemakers' unions and most of the others disappeared. Some printers' unions survived by becoming mutual benefit societies.
3. *1822-1827, Prosperity:* Unionism was revived and spread into other communities and industries.
4. *1829-1832, Depression:* Most local unions either disappeared or became quiescent. In New York and Philadelphia, workers actively became engaged in political reform movements.
5. *1833-1836, Prosperity:* The number of local unions significantly increased. In 1836, Philadelphia had 53 local unions; New York had 52; Baltimore had 23; and Boston had 16. The movement also spread westward; Pittsburgh had 13 locals; Cincinnati had 14; Louisville had 7. This period was the starting point of union organization on a substantial scale.

[12]*Ibid.*, I, p. 124.

[13]John R. Commons and associates: *History of Labour in the United States.* New York, Macmillan, 1918, I, pp. 127, 129.

[14]Lloyd G. Reynolds, *op. cit.*, pp. 46-47.

6. *1837-1849, Depression:* A complete industrial collapse occurred in 1837 with little economic recovery until the fifties.
   Trade unions almost completely disappeared from the scene.
7. *1850-1854, Prosperity:* Local union organizations spread
   rapidly, and several national trade unions were established
   which survive today. However, this growth was checked by
   slumps in 1855 and 1857.
8. *1863-1873, Prosperity:* This period of war and postwar prosperity saw local unions flourishing; the foundations for more
   national unions were established. Estimates indicate that
   total union membership was approximately 300,000 in 1872,
   distributed among 61 different trades.
9. *1873-1878, Depression:* The collapse of 1873 and the ensuing
   severe depression destroyed most of the local unions and
   many of the national organizations. Further estimates reveal
   that by 1878, union membership had fallen to some 50,000.
   However, it is significant that this depression did not completely destroy unionism as the earlier depressions had done.

THE ERA OF UPHEAVAL

The depression of the 1870's ushered in one of the most con-
fused periods in American labor history. Workers engaged in
violent protest over what they believed was ruthless exploitation
by employers. Demonstration occurred in many cities, often requiring forceful police intervention. Strikes among the miners
led to bloodshed and killing. In 1877, railway workers engaged
in a spontaneous uprising which caused widespread rioting, and
the country seemed to be facing a general labor insurrection.[15]

Even after these disturbances subsided, worker unrest and
dissatisfaction remained potentially explosive. In the 1880's, the
country again experienced the usual cycle of wage cuts and unemployment, attendant to a depression. So many strikes occurred
during this period that it is known as the "Great Upheaval."

At this time another element was introduced on the American
labor scene; foreign radicals, who entered this country as part of
the hordes of immigrants, arrived daily. These radicals sought
to impose upon American labor those socialistic and anarchistic
ideas then prevalent throughout Europe. Fear of their influence
colored many reports of unemployment demonstrations and pos-

15Foster R. Dulles, *op. cit.,* pp. 114-125.

sibly led to the tragic Haymarket Square Riot of 1886.[16] Although this tragedy did not have significant affect upon the labor movement, it did cast the shadow of radicalism and violence over it.

As the effects of the panic of 1873 deepened and widened, disorders occurred throughout the country. Crowds of unemployed workers gathered at huge meetings in New York, Chicago, Boston, Cincinnati, and Omaha to protest their intolerable situation. These homeless, hungry, and despairing workers refused to disperse on orders by the police, and violence erupted.[17] Similar unemployment riots and violence also occurred in the anthracite coal fields. However, this was only the prelude to the railroad strikes of 1877 which led to disorders and rioting that necessitated the intervention of federal troops to suppress them.[18]

The month of July 1877 was one of the most turbulent in American history. Its disorders and rioting had long-term consequences. The business community was aroused by the potential power of industrial workers; and, embarked upon an aggressive program to suppress all labor activity—reviving the old conspiracy laws, seeking to intimidate the workers from joining unions, imposing the "iron clad" oath, and enlisting strikebreakers when trouble threatened. Labor learned the lesson that both organization and authority were necessary to prevent strikes from becoming uncontrolled mob action which inevitably was suppressed by state or federal troops. As Professor Dulles sums it up, "Capitalism had won the first round of industrial strife, but was fearful of the future. Labor had lost, but it had a new realization of its latent strength."[19]

LABOR FEDERATIONS

Federation of national unions generally is considered to date from 1880's despite several abortive attempts at national federation in earlier years. Only three important federations have been

16Ernest B. Zeisler: *The Haymarket Riot*. Chicago, Alexander J. Isaacs, 1958, passim.

17Edward W. Martin: *The History of the Great Riots*. Philadelphia, National Publishing Company, 1877, passim.

18J. A. Dacus: *Annals of the Great Strikes*. St. Louis, Scammell and Co., 1877, passim.

19Foster R. Dulles, *op. cit.*, pp. 114-125.

formed primarily devoted to trade union objectives: the Knights of Labor, the American Federation of Labor, and the Congress of Industrial Organizations.

The Knights of Labor

The first of these, the Knights of Labor,[20] was founded by a group of workers in 1869 in Philadelphia. Originally, it was organized as a secret society with an elaborate ritual. Its members belonged to local assemblies, some of which included workers from a particular trade only or mixed assemblies including workers from various trades and industries. These local assemblies held membership in district assemblies that were federated into a national assembly. Overall organization largely was geographical in nature rather than by trade or industry. However, the union of all trades into a single labor organization was a cardinal objective of the Knights.

Also, wide divergence existed between theory and practice in this labor federation. Theoretically, the objectives were education, legislation, and the promotion of producer/consumer co-operation. Under a national leadership that was middle-class and mild,[21] local assemblies almost exclusively confined their activities to collective bargaining, using the strike to attain their objectives. Although the locals were to take no action without national consent, this proved to be purely theory. In practice, national officials were unable to exercise any control over the thousands of local assemblies scattered across the country. Locals functioned autonomously in their bargaining demands, strikes, and political activities.

The Knights of Labor grew slowly during the 1870's and increased rapidly during the prosperity of the early 1880's. The number of strikes in which they engaged also increased greatly, and most were successfully concluded. Membership peaked in 1886 at 700,000; but, from this point, the movement declined rapidly and never recovered. By 1890, membership had fallen

[20]Norman J. Ware: *The Labor Movement in the United States, 1860-1895.* New York, D. Appleton Co., 1929 passim.

[21]Terence V. Powderly: *Thirty Years of Labor.* Philadelphia, T. V. Powderly, 1890, passim.

to 100,000, and it continued to decline steadily thereafter.[22] Of the several reasons for this, one of the most paramount was the nature of its membership. Most members had no previous experience in unionism. They joined enthusiastically but were easily discouraged and quick to drop out. Consequently, the organization experienced a continuing high turnover in membership. Another discouraging factor was that most of the strikes conducted by the Knights after 1886 were lost as a partial result of the lack of central financing and direction. Finally, skilled members tended to withdraw and form national trade unions or to affiliate with the existing trade unions under the banner of the American Federation of Labor.

The American Federation of Labor

Initial steps for the formation of the American Federation of Labor[23] started in 1881, and the organization itself was established in 1886. It quickly assumed a leading role in the trade union movement because it was hard-hitting and its distinctive philosophy of trade unionism had a strong appeal to most organized workers. Its leaders were young, aggressive, and capable.[24] On May 1, 1886, these men led what was tantamount to a general strike. Some 340,000 workers demanded the eight-hour day, and approximately 190,000 workers obtained it as a result of this strike. These early AFL leaders also seem to have perfected a form of union organization which could withstand the test of time. While the Knights were declining, the membership of the national trade unions in the AFL doubled[25] between 1886 and 1894, increasing from 138,000 to 275,000.

One of the major reasons that the AFL grew and today remains in a position of predominance in the field of organized labor is the philosophy it espouses.[26] The first element in this trade union philosophy is group consciousness; interests of workers are

---

[22]Lloyd G. Reynolds, *op cit.*, p. 70.

[23]L. L. Lorwin: *The American Federation of Labor.* Washington, D. C., The Brookings Institute, 1933, passim.

[24]Samuel Gompers: *Seventy Years of Life and Labor.* New York, E. P. Dutton and Co., 1945, passim.

[25]Lloyd G. Reynolds, *op. cit.*, pp. 72-73.

[26]*Ibid.*

distinct from those of other groups. Next, the AFL is organized by trades; each craft has its own union. Early leaders also insisted that each national union be autonomous within its own field of operation. The federation serves as a confederation of sovereign bodies; its chief power is the granting of jurisdiction over particular trades or industries. The third cardinal principle in this philosophy is that the objectives of labor shall be pursued on the economic front through collective bargaining with employers. Almost from the outset, the AFL accepted the main tenets of the capitalist order: the purpose of unions is not to overthrow capitalism, but to obtain as much as possible for the workers within the existing system.

Thus, the AFL almost from the outset was an organizational model which was well-suited to the requirements of the skilled trades, thereby stimulating the formation of new national unions. It acted as a stabilizer of union membership during depression periods and presented a practical operating program which has proven highly successful in winning gains on the economic front.

Industrial Workers of the World

Between 1890 and 1935, Industrial Workers of the World (IWW)[27] was the only organization to arise and challenge the position of the AFL. This organization was formed in 1905 in Chicago by a small group of socialists and syndicalists from a number of national unions, notably the Western Federation of Miners. These men denounced the AFL in strong terms, because of its collaboration with employers, and put forth an extremely radical platform. Their objective was to win workers away from the AFL and to organize them in new industrial unions under IWW auspices.

Most of the socialists withdrew from the organization between 1906 and 1908. Those who remained largely were migratory workers from the western states who subscribed to the concept of direct action. Actual organizational structure of the union was decentralized to the point of chaos. Dues were very low and rarely collected. The federation virtually had no national treasury,

27P. F. Brissenden: *The I.W.W.* New York, Columbia University Press, 1920, passim.

and delegates "rode the rods" to national conventions. IWW had little success in wooing members from the AFL and never achieved a dues-paying membership in excess of 20,000 although the high turnover in membership actually meant that several hundred thousand workers passed through the organization during its existence.

Yet, the IWW was influential in two principal areas. The first of these was among the immigrant workers in the mass-production industries, who had either been neglected or actually injured when AFL crafts refused to support them during strikes. The area of operations was among the migratory agricultural, maritime, and lumber workers of the Middle West and the Far West. IWW tactics were well-suited to the needs of these workers, whose migratory existence made permanent local unions impossible. Also, the issues in dispute with an employer usually were so simple that bargaining experts were not needed. This organization reached the height of its influence immediately before the First World War. During the war, as well as in the postwar years, the IWW was severely persecuted by the Federal Government because of its anti-war and anti-capitalistic viewpoints. Many of its leaders were imprisoned; thus, this challenge to the AFL fell by the wayside.

On the other hand, the impact of the IWW on the total labor movement was important from the viewpoint that this revolutionary movement centered attention upon the desperate needs of vast numbers of unskilled workers and gave a new impetus to industrial unionism. However, the overwhelming majority of American workingmen remained as fundamentally opposed to IWW philosophy as were their employers or the middle class generally. AFL continued to dominate the labor movement, and revolutionary unionism made no real headway against business unionism. The IWW was a dramatic expression of left wing sentiment, but it made few converts. American labor could not be convinced that the historic role of the working class was to destroy capitalism.[28]

[28]Foster R. Dulles, *op cit.*, pp. 222-223.

The Congress of Industrial Organizations

The issue of craft versus industrial organization was discussed sporadically at AFL conventions from 1886 until the 1930's. Discussions grew into controversy and finally caused open conflict within the AFL. An insurgent revolt occurred, and the Committee for Industrial Organization was established. Issues in dispute were comparable to those existing when the AFL challenged the Knights of Labor some fifty years earlier: craft unionism versus industrial unionism. However, the valid basic areas of conflict soon became overshadowed in the quarrel between the AFL and the CIO and the power drives of rival leaders. These differences came to a climax in the national AFL conventions of 1934 and 1935. Industrial unionists were defeated at the 1935 convention; subsequently, they established the Committee for Industrial Organization. Not until 1938 did these insurgents form a permanent rival federation—the Congress of Industrial Organizations.[29]

Later success of the CIO organizing drives has become legend in trade union history.[30] During the late 1930's, one anti-union citadel after another capitulated. The list of employers whose companies were organized includes Ford, General Motors, Chrysler, General Electric, Westinghouse, United States Steel, Bethelehem Steel, Republic Steel, Goodyear, Firestone, major oil companies, larger radio and electrical equipment companies, the "big four" meatpackers, and numerous others.

These successes stemmed from a number of favorable conditions as well as the aggressive, well-financed organizing campaigns of the CIO. Probably, the most important factor was the existence of government administrations favorable to organized labor, both in Washington and in most of the industrialized states. Another was the National Labor Relations Act of 1935 which guaranteed the right to organize. Any employer who opposed the unionization of his workers by applying the customary techniques of espionage, black-listing, threats, and physical violence

---

[29]J. R. Walsh: *CIO: Industrial Unionism in Action.* New York, W. W. Norton & Co., 1937, passim.

[30]R. R. Brooks: *When Labor Organizes.* New Haven, Yale University Press, 1937, passim.

could be brought before the National Labor Relations Board and ordered to cease and desist from these activities, under threat of penalty. The Act itself also provided a new procedure for obtaining union recognition: the secret ballot.

A final important factor was the prolonged rise in business activity after 1933. Aside from some brief, minor setbacks, the economy moved rapidly to capacity operations and remained at this level throughout the 1940's and the early 1950's. This long period of prosperity enabled new unions to become thoroughly entrenched in their respective industries.

AFL-CIO Reunification

The ending of peace negotiations in 1937 between the AFL and CIO, which transformed the latter into a permanent organization, established a serious rival to the AFL. Therefore, from the very outset, the AFL subscribed to the need for reunifying the labor movement. Actually, both federations included similar union structures. The CIO did not exist exclusively of industrial unions. Ten of the 29 unions in the CIO in 1939 were craft organizations. Similarly, the AFL included industrial organizations.

A cardinal principle of the AFL, the autonomy of the internationals, became a cornerstone of the CIO. Much of the trade union philosophies remained common to both federations. First reunification efforts actually were undertaken in 1939 under President Franklin D. Roosevelt. However, the ultimate merger of the AFL and CIO did not take place until 1955. Leaders of this new federation envisioned a doubling of union membership within ten years and consequent increases in both economic and political power which would strengthen the security of all industrial workers. These bright expectations were not fulfilled because, at best, the AFL-CIO remained a federation of wholly autonomous individual unions. Its executive committee could only recommend action, rather than exercise any coercive power, when jurisdictional or other disputes threatened to block the course of reunification.[31]

Additionally, the AFL-CIO did not include all of the national

[31]Philip Taft, *op. cit.*, pp. 645-663.

or international unions. The Railway Brotherhoods and the United Mine Workers remained independent; and, within a few years, the Teamsters, the largest union in the country, was expelled due to internal corruption. Union membership failed to follow its historic growth trends, and the peak was achieved in 1956 with an overall total of 17,500,000 or 33.4 percent of the non-agricultural employment[32] (although the total had increased to 18,325,000 in 1966, this number represented only 28.8 percent of non-agricultural employment[33]). Numerous factors accounted for this situation, including unexpected obstacles to new organizing campaigns. In many areas little interest was manifested in unionization as a result of prosperity and the more generous wage policies instituted by enlightened employers. Outright opposition remained strong in geographic areas such as the South, where unions had never really obtained any foothold and organizers were hampered by state right-to-work laws. Probably, the most important consideration was a change in the structure of the civilian work force. The number of blue-collar workers, who made up the bulk of the union membership, was declining while the number of nonunion white-collar workers steadily rose. In traditional terms, the labor pool from which labor unions had drawn their membership was steadily shrinking. This meant that unions were forced to turn their attention to new fields and develop a way to effectively organize the growing number of workers who, for social rather than economic reasons, had always resisted unionism.

A membership of 15 million affiliated with the merged federation made it the largest labor group in the history of the United States and the free world, and the "preamble" to the constitution of the AFL-CIO expressed the attitude of the labor movement of 1955. It emphasized the fulfillment of the hopes and aspirations of the working people through collective bargaining and the "exercise of the rights and responsibilities of citizenship."[34] A class struggle declaration in the original AFL constitution and

[32]Foster R. Dulles, *op. cit.,* p. 379.

[33]*The American Almanac: The U. S. Book of Facts, Statistics, and Information 1970.* New York, Grosset & Dunlap, 1969, p. 236.

[34]Philip Taft: *op. cit.,* p. 661.

the emphasis upon industrial organization found in the CIO constitution each are absent. Today, the objectives and principles enunciated are in line with the traditional aspirations of organized labor in the United States. The federation aims to do the following:[35]

1. Aid workers to obtain improved wages, hours, and conditions of employment.
2. Assist affiliated unions.
3. Encourage affiliation of national and international unions with the federation.
4. Help workers irrespective of race, creed, or color to share the benefits of organization.
5. Seek to provide beneficial legislation for all the people and oppose that which is harmful.
6. Protect democratic institutions.
7. Promote the cause of peace and freedom.
8. Cooperate with and assist free and democratic labor movements in other countries.
9. Preserve and protect the autonomy of affiliates so that each abstains from raiding.
10. Encourage the sale of union-made goods.
11. Safeguard the democratic charter of the labor movement and protect the autonomy of each affiliated national and international union.
12. Encourage workers to register and vote in order to exercise their duties of citizenship.

All of these objectives might well be approved of by every trade unionist in the country. Aside from greater emphasis upon political action and explicit opposition to communism as well as corruption, the reunified AFL-CIO offered no surprises.

LABOR LEGISLATION

Labor legislation in this country started as early as 1630 when the General Court in Massachusetts undertook to enforce a wage ceiling of two shillings each day for carpenters, joiners, bricklayers, sawyers, thatchers, and other artisans.[36] It also established 18 pence for all day laborers, with the further provision that "all

---

[35]*Ibid.*, p. 662.
[36]Foster R. Dulles, *op. cit.*, pp. 11-13.

workmen shall worke the whole day, alloweing convenient tyme for food and rest." Forty years later, another law reaffirmed these general wage rates stating more specifically that the working day should be "10 houres in the daye besides repast," and extended its provisions to additional artisans.

Pre-Civil War

New Hampshire passed the first state 10-hour labor law in 1847. Pennsylvania adopted a bill the next year providing that no person should work more than a 10-hour day or 60-hour week "in cotton, woolen, silk, paper, bagging, and flax factories." During the 1850's, Maine, Connecticut, Rhode Island, Ohio, California, and Georgia adopted some versions of the 10-hour laws.[37]

The 1890's

By the 1890's, a Bureau of Labor Statistics had been established in the Federal Government, and comparable bureaus existed in 32 states. An Alien Contract Labor Law had been enacted and the Chinese Exclusion Acts were on the statute books. In 1898, President McKinley recommended the creation of an Industrial Commission. Various early state laws regulating certain phases of industrial activity were aimed toward improving working conditions in the mines and factories. However, unions remained in a poor position because the Sherman Act ban on combinations in restraint of trade was applied to them, along with the use of the injunction in suppressing strikes and boycotts.[38]

The Progressive Era

Moreover, Congress passed the Erdman Act in 1898. This act prohibited any discrimination against workers by the interstate railways due to union membership. Ten years later, the Supreme Court held that this provision of the Erdman Act was an invasion of both personal liberty and the rights of property. A comparable Kansas State statute also was outlawed in 1915, and the Supreme Court upheld an injunction which prohibited the United Mine Workers from seeking to organize employees who had been com-

---

[37]*Ibid.*, p. 86.
[38]*Ibid.*, p. 183.

pelled to agree not to join the union under "yellow-dog" contracts. Decisions upholding and enforcing yellow-dog contracts stood until passage of the Norris-LaGuardia Act of 1932, which finally reversed public policy.

During this period, the courts also sustained the employers in their counterattacks upon union boycotts. However, economic and social reforms also were enacted during the Progressive Era.[39] By 1912, 38 states had adopted child labor laws placing restrictions on the age at which children might be employed, limiting their hours of work, and otherwise safeguarding health and safety. Protection also was afforded to women in industry through legislation in 28 states where the maximum number of hours was set. At least 35 states had enacted workmen's compensation laws by 1915. These laws provided for compulsory payment of benefits for industrial accidents. Twenty-five states also enacted laws limiting the hours of work for men as well as women.

In 1914, Congress passed the Clayton Act which both strengthened earlier antitrust legislation and incorporated important clauses affecting the rights of labor. The new law stated that nothing in the antitrust laws should be construed to forbid the existence of unions, prevent them from lawfully carrying out their legitimate objectives, or to hold them to be illegal combinations or conspiracies in restraint of trade. It also outlawed the use of injunctions in all disputes between employers and employees "unless necessary to prevent irreparable injury to property, or to a property right . . . for which injury there is no adequate remedy at law."

Passage of the La Follette Seamen's Act in 1915 remedied many of the most glaring abuses in the employment of sailors and immeasurably improved conditions in the forecastles of American merchant vessels. A demand by railway workers for shorter hours was met the next year when the Adamson Act established an eight-hour day, with time-and-a-half for overtime for employees of all interstate railways. Finally, congressional enactment of a literacy test for all European immigrants in 1917 was a first step toward a policy of immigration restriction so long demanded by labor.

[39]*Ibid.*, pp. 196, 201-204.

The Norris-La Guardia Act

Moreover, early in March 1932, a highly significant victory for organized labor was won through the passage of the Norris-LaGuardia Act.[40] The measure declared as public policy the fact that labor should have full freedom of association, without interference by employers; outlawed yellow-dog contracts, and prohibited federal courts from issuing injunctions in labor disputes except under carefully defined conditions.

The New Deal

The advent of the New Deal[41] under Franklin D. Roosevelt proved to be a new and memorable era for American labor. Age-old traditions were smashed; new and dynamic forces were released. Greater gains were won by wage earners than in any previous period of United States history. Both the economic and political power of labor was immeasurably enhanced; the labor movement and unionization had clearly arrived.

The premise upon which New Deal policy toward labor was based already had been set forth in the general recognition of its right to organize as written into the Norris-LaGuardia Act. This was further expanded in the plan adopted and incorporated into the National Industrial Recovery Act. Industry was allowed to write its own codes of fair competition; and, in return, labor was provided with special safeguards for its interest. The Act stipulated that all industrial codes should contain three important provisions:

1. Employees should have the right to organize and bargain collectively through representatives of their own choosing, free from interference, restraint, or coercion on the part of employers.
2. No one seeking employment should be required to join a company union or to refrain from joining any labor organization of his own choosing.
3. Employers should comply with maximum hours, minimum rates of pay, and other conditions of employment approved by the President.

Two years after it was enacted, in May 1935, the National

40*Ibid.*, p. 263.
41*Ibid.*, pp. 264-267, 273-276, 281-285.

Industrial Recovery Act was declared unconstitutional by the Supreme Court. However, on July 5, 1935, the Wagner Act (the National Labor Relations Act) became law. This statute upheld the right of wage earners to organize without making any corresponding concessions to management. Every unfair labor practice banned in the Wagner Act applied to employers, and it imposed no restraints upon the unions. The administration of the act was placed in the hands of a new National Labor Relations Board.

Protection given labor in its right to organize and bargain collectively was the most important phase of the pro-labor policy that was generally followed under the New Deal. In addition to the Wagner Act, Roosevelt provided the Works Progress Administration, the Social Security Act, the Walsh-Healey Public Contracts Act (established the 40-hour week and minimum wages for all employees of contractors making supplies for the Government), and the Fair Standards Act. In 1938, the latter provided for a minimum wage of 25 cents per hour, rising to 40 cents per hour in seven years; a 44-hour week, to be reduced to 40-hours in three years; and prohibited the labor of children under 16 in industries whose products entered into interstate commerce.

Restrictive Trends

Conversely, World War II called for the subordination of industrial worker concerns in the national interest. The key to labor's wartime history was an agency created to implement agreements reached at a labor-management conference called by President Roosevelt immediately following Pearl Harbor. This agency was the National War Labor Board.[42]

Rising prices, induced by the inflationary pressures of wartime, led unions to demand wage increases that were at least commensurate with the rise in the cost of living, and they threatened to strike to obtain their demands. The Board sought some sort of formula which would hold wages in line, while allowing increases that were clearly justified by the rise in cost of living. In July 1942, the Little Steel companies demanded a wage increase of one dollar per day. After lengthy hearings, the decision

---

[42]*Ibid.*, **pp.** 339-340, 352, 356-360, 365-366, 381-382.

was that a wage increase was justified, but that it should be equivalent to the increase in living costs only—44 cents per day. The Little Steel formula became the basic yardstick for settling all wartime wage disputes.

In addition, the Economic Stabilization Act, passed in October 1942, directed the Board to restrict all wage increases (except where flagrantly substandard conditions existed) to the 15 percent increase in straight-line hourly wages that had been granted in the steel industry. Consequently, for the remainder of the war, the National War Labor Board had two distinct functions: settlement of dispute cases and supervision of voluntary wage agreements.

Furthermore, a strike in the coal mines and other work stoppages in the spring of 1943 brought about the passage of the Smith-Connally bill which empowered the President to take over the control of any plant or industry when government mediation in a labor dispute proved unsuccessful and any halt in production threatened the war effort. Once under government jurisdiction, criminal penalties could be enforced against any persons who instigated or promoted a strike. Additionally, union contributions to political campaign funds were expressly forbidden.

Altogether during the war years, the War Labor Board imposed settlements in 17,650 dispute cases affecting over 12 million employees; and, in 95 percent of these cases successfully averted any further threat to production. It also approved 415,000 voluntary wage agreements involving approximately 20 million workers.

A wave of postwar labor agitation and strikes resulted in the passage of the Taft-Hartley Act in June of 1947. This was a long and immensely complicated measure having the declared purpose of restoring equality in bargaining power between employees and employers which, it was contended, had been sacrificed in the Wagner Act. The rights guaranteed labor in the Wagner Act were matched by specific safeguards for the rights of management. Employers were granted full freedom of expression in respect to their views regarding union organization, short of threats of reprisal or promises of benefits; and, they were authorized to call for elections to determine the appropriate bargaining units in wage negotiations. At the same time, the legislation defined as unfair labor practice the actions of unions which in any way were an attempt at coercion of employers, engaging in either secondary boycotts or jurisdictional strikes, or refusing to bargain collectively.

The law also incorporated a number of provisions directly affecting union security. It expressly banned the closed shop, required highly complicated voting procedures for establishing the union shop, and left the door open to even more severe anti-union legislation by the states. In fact, this provision made possible the so-called state "right-to-work" laws.

Further restrictions provided that unions were required to give a 60-day notice for the termination or modification of any agreement and were suable in the federal courts for breach of contract. They were not allowed to make contributions or otherwise expend any of their funds in political campaigns. Their officers were required to file affidavits affirming that they were not members of the Communist Party or of any organization supporting it. It also empowered the President, after making an investigation through a special board of inquiry, to apply for an 80-day injunction against any strike that imperiled the national health or safety. Finally, Taft-Hartley made a number of significant changes in existing legislation. It provided for the enlargement of the National Labor Relations Board and established an independent Federal Mediation and Conciliation Service with authority to step into any labor dispute that threatened a substantial interruption of interstate commerce.

After Taft-Hartley, various incidents of union corruption that occurred throughout the mid-1950's resulted in the Landrum-Griffin Act, adopted by Congress in September of 1959. The first sections of this law dealt with the corruption issue and incorporated a Bill of Rights for union members. These provisions embodied specific safeguards for democratic procedures in the conduct of union affairs, protected union funds with the imposition of fines and prison sentences for any official guilty of their misuse, made any forceful interference with the rights of union members a federal offense, and prohibited persons convicted of certain crimes (as well as members of the Communist Party) from serving as union officials for five years after their release from prison or after termination of Communist membership.

It also severely tightened many of the Taft-Hartley provisions governing union activities.

For example, the existing ban on secondary boycotts was broadened to prevent a union from bringing any pressure to bear upon an employer to make him cease doing business with another employer. A new curb was placed on picketing to outlaw any action whereby a union sought to coerce a company where a rival union was lawfully recognized. It also broadened state jurisdiction.

The 1960's

In 1961,[43] the Fair Labor Standards Act was amplified to cover an increased number of workers and to raise the minimum wage to $1.25 per hour. Apart from legislation extending the social security program and raising minimum wages, a Manpower Development and Training Act was passed in 1962. This measure was intended to assist Workers who had lost their jobs due to displacement by machines. Subsequently, Congress passed the Economic Opportunity Act, which provided a job corps for young people, work-training assistance, and varied community action programs.

SOME CLOSING OBSERVATIONS

Obviously, the foregoing capsulated treatment of the labor movement in the United States merely touches upon the major highlights in the mainstream of trade union development. It does not account for the independent unions which currently exercise significant influence on the American scene nor those that played a transient role. No consideration has been given to vagaries in labor legislation experienced at the state level. However, despite these shortcomings, it serves to illustrate the driving objectives as well as consistency of the American labor movement. It is from this base that organized labor has reached into the ranks of public employees and continues to grow in strength, as well as recognition in this area, as discussed in Chapter III.

In summary, organized labor—as we know it in the United

[43]*Ibid.*, pp. 394-416.

States today—was shaped by the social, economic, and political conditions existing throughout its history. The majority of these unions concentrate their activity upon protecting their members in the place of employment.

As a result of the organized labor efforts, American workers enjoy rights at their place of employment that are equal or superior to those workers in any other country in the world. Unions continue to follow a policy of "more and more" in matters of wages.

The labor movement of today is decidedly different from the one that existed in the early 1930's. Its numbers are approximately six times as great; and, it operates its legal, political, and research activities at a greatly expanded level. It shows a much greater and continuing interest in foreign affairs and international labor. It also is concerned with a greater variety of legislative problems and public issues. Despite these great changes, it clearly shows the influence of the labor movement of the past. Its major interest remains the improvement in conditions of employment within the established institutional framework. As in the past, unions remain largely powerless, except for delaying actions, against the erosions of their positions by technical innovations (automation). Relieving unemployment generated by such changes always has been and remains beyond the power of labor unions, although they have made some contributions in the area through labor-management arrangements. Yet, like the level of employment in general, the reabsorption of the technically displaced, their training, and offsets to wage losses must, now and in the future, be the primary responsibility of government.[44]

[44]Philip Taft, *op. cit.*, pp. 708-709.

Chapter III

DEVELOPMENT OF PUBLIC
EMPLOYEE/POLICE UNIONS

Unionism in the public sector had its origins in the late 1800's. Although governmental agencies were small, communications poor, and unions in the private sector were embryonic, the first public employees' organizations emerged among postal employees, policemen, and teachers.

Early in the 1900's, policemen were organized in 37 cities, including Boston, Los Angeles, Portland (Oregon), St. Paul, and Jersey City.[1] Yet, to the public, the policemen was the embodiment of civic authority, the official guardian of law and order, and the living symbol of governmental power. His alliance with the purveyors of collective bargaining seemed, to most, to be an attack upon the very foundations of the state. As a consequence, strong hostility towards the idea of police unions existed, especially those aligned with organized labor. In Washington, policemen were ordered to resign from their union.[2] Nevertheless, police unionism remained on the rise until the 1919 strike of policemen in Boston; following this, police unions all but disappeared for almost twenty-five years. However, this has not prevented the police from remaining one of the most thoroughly organized groups of American employees. Almost every city has some kind of policemen's association, some of which trace their history back to pre-Civil War days.

BENEVOLENT ASSOCIATIONS

Most of these originally were benevolent associations. These associations were founded early to protect the policeman and to improve his working conditions. Fortunately for the organizers,

[1]Philip Taft, *op. cit.*, p. 348.
[2]*Ibid.*

they existed with little official opposition because they functioned in such manner as to give little offense to police hierarchies. Many were even controlled by high ranking police officials, and it appeared to be common policy to seek their ends through departmental favor or through the power of the political machine. The military-like organization of the police force made it especially easy for the department to control the association, while the power exerted by the policeman on his beat made him a valuable ally of the political machine. As one historian put it:[3]

> Capitalizing on this strategic position, the police, working hand in glove with corrupt municipal politics, acquired a degree of political power far greater than that of any other class of American municipal workers.

Additionally, it was common in the early and mid-1900's for police associations to maintain "slush funds" which were administered by "legislative agents" who were hired because of their knowledge and abilities to spend the money "so it would do the most good." As a result, legislators, who were jealous of their reputations, often refused to handle police measures. For example, in Chicago, during the consideration of the police budget of 1910, police pressure upon the aldermen was so persistent that the city council was compelled to hold its sessions behind closed doors. A charge was voiced that the United Police of Chicago had collected $60,000 from its 4,000 members to buy the votes of aldermen who were opposing a salary increase. An investigation of these charges was instituted; and, during the course of the investigation, the president of the United Police disappeared with a large part of the funds. He was subsequently caught, convicted, and the United Police was disbanded.[4]

Earlier in New York, the police commissioner also charged that the Patrolmen's Benevolent Association had a large slush fund locked in its safe. After much haggling and the obtaining of a court order, the safe was opened; it revealed an amount far in excess of the originally estimated $20,000.[5]

[3]Sterling D. Spero: *Government As Employer.* New York, Remsen Press, 1948, p. 246.
[4]Chicago City Council, *Proceedings,* January 26, 1913.
[5]Sterling D. Spero, *op. cit.,* p. 247.

The New York Patrolmen's Benevolent Association had been formed in 1894, but it was not until 1914 that the organization and the city administration came into open conflict. Confrontation occurred over the so-called "Goethals Bill" which would have abolished the right of policemen to appeal to the courts in case of removal, substituting a hearing before the commissioner and an administrative board. The measure was defeated primarily because of efforts of the Association, and the right of judicial review of removals was maintained. It is interesting to note, however, that this fight changed the tactics of the Patrolmen's Benevolent Association. Open methods were soon substituted for secret and underground activity, and attempts were made to win the support of the press and public opinion for all legislation proposed at City Hall or in the state capital.

THE WORLD WAR I ERA

Moreover, the rise in prices about the time that the United States entered World War I helped to change the New York policeman's attitude, because he suffered particularly. In addition to his ordinary living expenses, he was required to make a large outlay for uniforms, arms, and equipment. He could not, like others workers, wear shabby or worn-out clothes. His standards remained unchanged although prices soared and his salary stayed the same.

In spite of the generally admitted justice of the policemen's claims, efforts to raise salaries usually met with stiff opposition from city administrations. Even a small increase to policemen amounted to a large item in the city budget. For example, $100 a year to each of New York's patrolmen meant a total increase of nearly $1,500,000. Also, an increase to the police usually meant a similar increase to the firemen.

Elsewhere in the nation, unrest and discontent among all classes of public employees grew rapidly during the fall and winter of 1917. One group after another, including the police, turned to the organized labor movement, believing it to be a thoroughly effectual way to correct their grievances. Federal employees formed a national union affiliated with the American Federation of Labor. Old, conservative organizations such as the

National Association of Letter Carriers and the Railway Mail Association threw in their lot with organized labor. Teachers' unions were being formed all over the country. The unionization of firemen had spread so rapidly that plans were being made for the formation of a firemen's international within the American Federation of Labor.[6]

The police also were affected. Associations in several cities applied for union charters from the American Federation of Labor, but the executive council rejected all applications on the basis of an 1897 ruling refusing the admission of an organization of private police in Cleveland. This ruling declared that it was "not within the province of the trade-union movement" to organize policemen on the ground that they were "too often controlled by forces inimical to the labor movement."[7] However, the policemen persisted in their demands; and, when the Federation assembled in convention in November 1917, it consented to ask the executive council to reconsider the ruling of twenty years earlier and report its recommendations to a subsequent convention.

While this matter was pending, police demands for higher salaries grew even more insistent. In New York City, patrolmen and firemen were receiving from $1,050 to $1,500 per year; they demanded an increase. Their representative declared in May 1918:[8]

> If the patrolmen and firemen were employees of a private corporation instead of the City of New York, their demands for salary increase would be enforced by a strike just as organized labor on the railroads and elsewhere has compelled recognition. But the patrolmen and firemen do not even think of a strike. They are loyal to the city but they expect the city shall do for them this year what the corporations are compelled to do for employees who have less ground upon which to base an appeal.

When the city raised salaries to about half of what was being demanded, the firemen, against whom the American Federation of Labor placed no barriers, joined the official labor movement by affiliating with the International Association of Fire Fighters.

[6]*Ibid.*, p. 248.
[7]American Federation of Labor, *Proceedings*, 1897, p. 43.
[8]*The Chief*, May 25, 1918, p. 1.

In September 1918, the police of Cincinnati went on strike. Drastic action was taken only after the authorities had persisted for months in ignoring the men's demands for an annual pay increase of from $1,260 to $1,500. When all but 48 members of the force refused to report for duty, 600 home guardsmen immediately were sent to take their places. The next day, guardsmen were assisted by boy scouts serving as traffic officers. Although great crowds gathered on the streets because of a parade of 25,000 drafted soldiers, no disorder and no confusion resulted. After three days, the men returned to duty with the assurance that no striker would be punished. Even though no public promises were made regarding salaries, all interested parties understood that the men's demands would be met as soon as possible. Within a few months, salaries were raised to $1,500.[9]

THE BOSTON POLICE STRIKE

While events were taking place in Cincinnati, Boston policemen and firemen were also waging a vigorous joint campaign for higher pay. At the peak of the campaign, firemen affiliated with the International Association of Fire Fighters and voted to strike if their demands were not met. The strike order was rescinded only after city authorities had given definite promise of relief. Two months later, in November 1918, the city finance commission recommended a $100 annual increase for both firemen and police. In its report, the commission declared:[10]

> The members of the police department were doubtless as desirous of an increase in their salary as the firemen, but with better spirit of fair play to their city and to their own reputation, refused to a man to support coercion measures upon the city authorities.

Yet, throughout the previous summer—while the salary campaign was in progress—constant talk of unionizing the police was heard, although the American Federation of Labor still barred them from membership. Rumors were so persistent that the police commissioner declared in his general orders:[11]

[9]Sterling D. Spero, *op. cit.*, p. 253.
[10]*Boston Herald,* November 20, 1918.
[11]*Report of the Commissioner of Police for the City of Boston,* 1920, p. 9.

I cannot believe that a proposition to turn the police force into a union . . . will ever be formally presented to its members, but if, unfortunately, such a question should ever arise, I trust that it will be answered with an emphatic refusal . . .

The $100 increase failed to quiet unrest among the police. It was half what the men had demanded and would only cover the cost of official equipment. Subsequently, the police sent a committee from their organization, the Boston Social Club, to see the mayor and demand a full $200. They warned him that, unless adjustments were made, they would be compelled to leave the force and accept better paying jobs. They also said that the service would become demoralized because new men would not be attracted by the wages offered. The mayor was unimpressed. "In view of the serious financial condition of the city," he said, ". . . here is a limit beyond which we cannot go."[12]

Strike talk was soon revived, but the possibility of a walkout was denied everywhere. At this time, the police commissioner died and was replaced by a hard line advocate, Edwin U. Curtis, who began his official career with the following announcement:[13]

Any member of the police department who is so dissatisfied that he cannot perform his work faithfully, honestly, and cheerfully, pending the decision regarding the requested salary increase, may resign. **1759100**

That same day, the Boston Social Club unanimously decided not to accept less than the $200 increase. Many of the 700 men who voted on the question said they would resign from the force in the event that the demand was not met.

A few days later, a committee from the Police Social Club called on the new commissioner to discuss the situation. Although the previous commissioner had recognized the Social Club as the official spokesman for the force, had received its delegates, and listened to their suggestions—Commissioner Curtis refused to continue this practice despite the growing dissatisfaction of the men. Instead, he instituted a central grievance committee composed of delegates elected from the various stations. The elections were not honest; it was common knowledge that the name of one

[12]*Boston Herald*, December 24, 1918.
[13]*Boston Herald*, December 31, 1918.

man was sent to headquarters as a delegate who was not elected by the employees.[14]

A few weeks later, Commissioner Curtis further aggravated the situation by forbidding the police to appear before the Legislature in behalf of measures of interest to them, unless they first received his permission. This was a matter of real importance in the salary campaign; for, under this order, the police were forbidden to lobby for an increase in the city tax rate in the event that this was needed to ensure their receiving the higher pay.

Meanwhile, soaring prices were making inadequate the minimum demand of $200. The city council sent a committee to the mayor seeking some solution, but the mayor reiterated his original stand that nothing could or would be done. Then Commissioner Curtis entered the controversy, declaring the reasonableness of the demands and urging that the policemen be given the $200 increase. Two months later the mayor consented to a compromise; the maximum salary was to be increased by $200 to a level of $1,600, while the men in the lower grades were to receive advances of $100 each.[15]

This caused so much confusion and dissatisfaction that, four days later, the mayor granted the demands in full—adding that he had no idea where the city would get the money.[16] New scale entrance salaries were $1,100, and the maximum reached $1,600. However, by then, these increases already were inadequate because of spiraling costs.

A few weeks later, the American Federation of Labor met in convention and lifted the twenty-year-old barrier against the chartering of police unions. President Gompers said, in discussing the step:[17]

> For years and years, the members of the police force of the various cities throughout the country have made application to be organized unions, to have their clubs and associations transferred from their then existing character to become unions . . . The

[14]Marion C. Nichols: The Boston police system. *The Christian Register,* October 1919, p. 493.

[15]*Boston Evening Transcript,* May 14, 1919.

[16]*Boston Herald,* May 18, 1919.

[17]*Hearings,* Committee on the District of Columbia, United States Senate, 66th Congress, 1st Session, September 1919, p. 110.

policemen have appealed to our representatives in various cities and have appealed to me, coming clandestinely and secretively for fear that they might be seen and spotted and victimized, as many of them have, to try to get them some relief in a way that they cannot get in their existing form of organization.

Response to the Federation's new policy was astonishing. Within nine weeks after the adjournment of the convention, 65 police organizations applied for charters. Thirty-three were granted to unions with a total membership of 2,265. By September of 1919, 37 locals had been chartered. The growth of these, after admission to the Federation, brought their membership to approximately 4,000, exclusive of the unions in Canada where the movement included the police of Montreal, Toronto, and others of the most important cities of the Dominion.[18] Gompers further commented.[19]

I have been President of the American Federation of Labor for thirty-six out of the thirty-nine years of its existence. In all those years I have never seen or heard nor has there come under my observation in any form so many appeals, so many applications for charters from any given trade or calling, business or profession, in so short a time as were received by the American Federation of Labor from policemen's unions.

The Federation did nothing to induce policemen to join its ranks. All of the initiative came from the policemen themselves.[20] In dozens of cities, including New York and Chicago where no formal steps to secure charters were taken, labor sentiment was on the rise, and the issue of affiliation preoccupied the men.

Local authorities received the moment in various ways, ranging from extreme hostility to outright approval. In Oklahoma City, the policemen's union—100 percent strong—had the full support of the mayor.[21] In a few other places, pro-labor officials also encouraged unionization; but, in most cities, the union was accepted grudgingly as an inevitable development of the times. Affiliation was effected; authorities protested; but, little happened.

18Sterling B. Spero, *op. cit.*, p. 256.
19Congressional Hearings, September 1919, *op. cit.*
20*Ibid.*
21*Ibid.*, p. 111.

Near the end of July 1919, a petition for a union charter was circulated among the policemen of Boston. When this came to the attention of Commissioner Curtis, he declared, "I feel that it is my duty to say that I disapprove of the movement on foot. . . ."[22] Aside from one paper which made no comment, the Boston press also was unanimous in its disapproval of the policemen's union plans.

Up to this juncture, the Commissioner merely disapproved of unionization; he had not forbidden it. Other public officials had repeatedly disapproved of the unionization of their employees in a manner similar to private employers. However, this disapproval was never interpreted as depriving employees of their right to organize, if they so desired. The postmaster had repeatedly condemned unions in strong terms, but postal employees continued to maintain their unions.

Accordingly, the Boston police continued with their plans, and the Social Club voted to ask the American Federation of Labor for a union charter. On August 8, 1919, the men were informed that their charter had been granted. It was received the next day.

On August 11, with the union an established fact, Police Commissioner Curtis issued the following order:[23]

No member of the force shall join or belong to any organization, club or body composed of present or present and past members of the force which is affiliated with or a part of any organization, club or body outside the department, except that a post of the Grand Army of the Republic, the United Spanish War Veterans, and the American Legion of World War Veterans may be formed within the department.

Strictly speaking, the broad and sweeping character of the order made its legal validity questionable. However, everyone knew that it was aimed at the policemen's union and that it would not be used for any other purpose than to destroy that union.

The union hired counsel, who considered the possibility of enjoining the commissioner from interfering with their organiza-

[22]Report of Police Commissioner for Boston, 1920, *op. cit.*, p. 258.
[23]Sterling B. Spero, *op. cit.*, p. 258.

tion on the grounds that such action was in violation of the law of the state. The law read, in part:[24]

> No person shall himself or by his agents coerce or compel a person into written or oral agreement not to join or become a member of a labor organization as a condition of securing employment or continuing in employment of such person.

The Commissioner contended that policemen were not "employees," but officers of the state. He also expressed willingness to have the validity of his rule tested in the courts. If the decision should be adverse to his contention that the police officers were public officers, he admitted that his rule then would be invalid and that any man discharged for its violation would be reinstated.[25] "But he made clear that he made no intimation," declared an interviewer, "that any member of the police force who denying the rule's validity abandons his duty by a strike or walkout would not be reinstated if discharged for that reason, even if he had the power to reinstate."[26]

This statement followed shortly upon the announcement that the Commissioner had ordered the printing of 1,000 discharge blanks and another 1,000 suspension forms.

The union ignored this clear intimation that the Commissioner intended to "go the limit" in his efforts to keep the police force out of the organized labor movement. On the day following the above mentioned announcement the union met, elected officers, and effected a permanent organization.

Three days later, the Central Labor Union of Boston met and welcomed the policemen's union into its ranks. "We urge them," it resolved, "to maintain their position and promise to them every atom of support that organized labor can bring to bear in their behalf in the event that they should need such support." Newspapers interpreted this as a general strike threat in case the police walked out,[27] and this resolution probably encouraged the police to continue with their efforts; but, when it came to the real test, organized labor of Boston deserted the policemen and reneged

[24]Massachusetts, Acts of 1919, Chapter 514, Section 19.
[25]*Boston Evening Transcript*, August 20, 1919.
[26]*Boston Herald*, August 20, 1919.
[27]*Boston Herald*, August 18, 1919.

on their solemn pledge. Patrolmen received no tangible assistance and were compelled to carry the fight alone.

The following week, the Commissioner filed charges against eight policemen who had been selected as officers of the union. Shortly afterward, eleven others were added. In addition, the mayor issued a statement regarding the charges:[28]

> The issue between the commissioner and the policemen is clearcut. It is a question of whether the policemen have a right to form a union and become affiliated with the American Federation of Labor . . .
> The American Federation of Labor deserves our cooperation and support in every proper way, but I do not think the policemen of any of our states or municipalities should become affiliated with it. This is, as I understand it, Commissioner Curtis' attitude and I think he is right.

The right to affiliate with the labor movement now overshadowed all other issues between the policemen and the commissioner. However, the real issues were low pay, long hours, and unsatisfactory channels of communication between the department and the force; these were the grievances that the patrolmen were depending upon the new union to correct.

Next, the mayor appointed a committee of 34 citizens, composed of leading financial and business representatives, to investigate the entire situation and, if possible, effect a settlement. Its first action was to issue a statement declaring that the policemen should not affiliate with the American Federation of Labor.[29] However, for the next three days, a subcommittee was in constant consultation with city officials and counsel for the policemen's union. On the fourth day, an announcement was made which stated that the executive committee believed that an adjustment could be worked out whereby the men would give up their American Federation of Labor charter and, at the same time, obtain better working conditions.

Up to this point, the commissioner appeared friendly and willing to cooperate. Now, this attitude changed to one of hos-

---

28*Ibid.*

29*Report of the Committee Appointed by Mayor Peters to Consider the Police Situation* (Document 108, 1919), p. 2.

tility; he appointed a prominent corporation lawyer as his special counsel. Fearing that a strike was imminent because of this move, the mayor's committee consulted with the union and drew up the following plan:[30]

(1) That the police surrender their American Federation of Labor charter but maintain their union as an independent organization.

(2) That present wages, hours and working conditions require material adjustment and should be investigated by a committee of three citizens who shall forthwith be selected by the concurrent action of the mayor, the commissioner, and the Policemen's Union and their conclusions communicated to the mayor and the police commissioner, and that hereafter all questions arising relating to hours and wages and physical conditions of work which the Policemen's Union desires to bring before the commissioner shall be taken up with the police commissioner by the duly accredited officers and committees of the Boston Policemen's Union and should any difference arise thereto which cannot be adjusted it shall be submitted to three citizens of Boston selected by agreement between the mayor, the police commissioner, and the Boston Policemen's Union. The conclusions of the three citizens thus selected shall be communicated to the citizens of Boston by publication. The provisions of this section shall not apply to any question of discipline.

Subsequent clauses provided for no discrimination against any policeman who joined or failed to join the independent union and that no member of the force should be discriminated against because of any previous affiliation with the American Federation of Labor.

The plan was submitted to the mayor and won his approval. It also was submitted to the police commissioner who rejected the proposal and proceeded to find 19 men guilty of violating his order. They were formally suspended from the service. The mayor was then powerless to act; while the police department was paid by the municipality, it was administered by the commissioner who was appointed by the governor (Calvin Coolidge).

Therefore, the predicted consequences followed rapidly. A meeting was called by the policemen's union, and the members declared that they were as guilty as the 19 men who the commis-

[30]*Ibid.,* pp. 19-20.

sioner had disciplined. They voted by 1,134 to two for a strike, to start in the afternoon of September 9, 1919. Actually, this step was not taken to force higher pay or better working conditions or to compel the recognition of the right to organize and affiliate with the American Federation of Labor. It was a demonstration of loyalty to the 19 men who had committed no greater wrong than their 1,100 fellows who belonged to the union but had not been tried for violating orders.

That night the leading members of the citizen's committee and the mayor met with the governor who was urged to accept the committee's plan or to take steps to ensure the protection of the city when the police left their posts. Governor Coolidge refused to intervene, despite repeated appeals. It thus became apparent that the only persons, aside from the police themselves, who were in a position to prevent a strike had no intention of doing so. Therefore, the mayor and his committee then turned their attention to ensuring the safety of the city. However, despite assurances to the contrary, no reserves of any significance were available for 14 hours after the strike. During this period, the city experienced extensive property damage, along with looting; and, seven people were killed in riots.[31]

No one was willing to admit that failure to provide for the protection of Boston on the night of the walkout was a deliberate attempt to use the inevitable disorder as a strike-breaking weapon. Every responsible party tried to dodge the blame for smashing police unionism at the expense of the lives and property of the people of Boston.

Thus, public support of the authorities in their stand against the strike was widespread and powerful. President Wilson referred to the strike as "an intolerable crime against civilization."[32] Hundreds of letters and telegrams of congratulations were received by Governor Coolidge. Resolutions of endorsement and aid came from the Massachusetts Chamber of Commerce, the Boston Bar Association, the American Legion State Executive Committee, the Masonic Grand Lodge of Massachusetts, the New England Shoe and Leather Association, the Massachusetts Press

---

[31]Sterling D. Spero, *op. cit.,* pp. 269-276.
[32]David Ziskind, *op. cit.,* p. 47.

Association, the Women's Anti-Suffrage Association of Massachusetts and many other organizations. All of the Boston daily newspapers denounced the strike, and the *Christian Science Monitor* carried editorials from various papers throughout the country—all adverse to the policemen.

The Boston police strike ended after four days, with the 1,200 striking policemen being summarily dismissed from the force.[33] Despite lengthy litigation, none were ever rehired nor did they collect past benefits.[34] Subsequently, Calvin Coolidge made his famous statement regarding the right of police to strike—a statement oft-quoted today as the basis for denying the police any right to unionize. He said, "There is no right to strike against the public safety by anybody, anytime, anywhere."[35]

The effects of the Boston police strike were not confined to that city. In other Massachusetts towns—New York City, in Washington, D. C., and elsewhere—authorities hastened to give or promise pay increases to their policemen in an effort to make certain of their loyalty. In all the cities where policemen had organized, a powerful opposition to the unions arose that ultimately led to the dissolution of all American Federation of Labor affiliations.

Much speculation has occurred as to the extent to which the activity of Governor Calvin Coolidge in the Boston police strike aided him in obtaining the Presidency of the United States. It is certain that most of the circumstances of the strike were never generally known and that his repute for saving the city, though entirely unfounded, was widespread.

Regardless of speculation, however, the immediate results of the Boston police strike can be accurately and briefly summarized. The smashing of a union, the loss of jobs by some 1,200 men, the tremendous cost of maintaining 4,000 guardsmen on duty, the destruction and theft of property, the loss of several lives, and the generation of social hatreds can be listed on the liability side. Increased wage scale and free uniforms for the new police-

[33]M. W. Aussieker, Jr.: *Police Collective Bargaining.* Chicago, Public Personnel Association, Public Employee Relations Library No. 18, 1969, p. 1.
[34]*Ibid.*
[35]*Ibid.*

men can be listed as assets—a tragic boxscore that could have been prevented.

AFTERMATH OF THE BOSTON POLICE STRIKE

Historically, the Boston police strike was not treated as a labor dispute. It was handled as a revolt against public authority, an attempted political upheaval. Yet the affair does clearly demonstrate the advantages that authorities possess in a dispute with their employees, especially those engaged in the performance of vital public safety functions.

Actually, the members of the Boston Policemen's Union, despite losing their jobs, won the strike for their successors. Other than this, the strike resulted in making Calvin Coolidge an unwarranted national hero and in a complete destruction of the policemen's trade union movement. Few people doubt that, if the Boston episode had not occurred, the police would have been as well-organized within the labor movement as firemen.

In almost every city, police employees gave up their organization without a great amount of protest. This is interesting because the principal reason for opposing the affiliation of police with the American Federation of Labor was the danger of a strike; yet, no strike of unionized police and no serious threat of one occurred outside of Boston.

Yet, for some twenty years, the police union movement lay dormant. It wasn't until both the American Federation of Labor and the Congress of Industrial Organizations turned their organizing efforts into the field of public employees in the 1940's that the movement finally revived (these activities are discussed in the ensuing sections).

AMERICAN FEDERATION OF STATE, COUNTY AND MUNICIPAL EMPLOYEES (AFSCME)

The dormancy of police unionization activity was broken when the American Federation of State, County and Municipal Employees (AFSCME) charted its first police local in Portsmouth, Virginia in 1937.[36] A few years later it took on a concerted drive

36*Ibid.*, p. 2.

for police membership in the face of warnings of disaster based upon the Boston experience. By the end of 1944, the Federation reported 31 police locals, 17 of which were established during that year.[37] By the end of 1946, it further reported 36 locals composed wholly of policemen and an additional 33 in which policemen were members, along with other groups of municipal employees. Included in both categories were such cities as Hartford, Connecticut; Springfield, Illinois; Tacoma, Washington; New Britain, Connecticut; Omaha, Nebraska; and St. Paul and Duluth, Minnesota. Some locals were organized in county sheriff's departments and some among state highway and traffic police. All of the police, whether in separate or mixed locals, were bound by no-strike charter provisions.[38] (The 1970 International Convention amended the AFSCME Constitution to remove the strike prohibition applicable to law enforcement officers—see Appendix A for a copy of the amendment).

On the other hand, the AFSCME movement met with resistance. In 38 cities, attempts to form unions were stopped by local authorities at the very beginning.[39] Elsewhere, when locals actually got under way, they were broken up and forced to sever their outside affiliations.

In Chicago, for example, a police union affiliated with the AFSCME was organized in 1944, but an opinion of the corporation counsel denied the right of the union to exist and informed the commissioner that he possessed "the power to prohibit police officers from becoming members of a labor union." The commissioner then issued an order banning such membership, and the policemen "backed down."[40]

A year earlier (1943) a police local chartered in Los Angeles was attacked by the police chief, the mayor, city council, and the local newspapers. However, the union continued to quietly build its membership; and, in 1944, it engaged in an effort to raise salaries and claimed credit for obtaining an increase in the basic

---

[37]*Ibid.*

[38]Sterling D. Spero, *op. cit.*, p. 289.

[39]Carl E. Heustis: Police unions. *Journal of Criminal Law, Criminology and Police Science,* Vol. 48, November 1958, p. 4.

[40]Sterling D. Spero, *op. cit.*, p. 290.

pay. For two years, it witnessed a relationship of grudging acceptance by city council to include it in the payroll deduction plan. This brought a stinging veto message from the mayor in which he said:[41]

> I feel that a police union has no place in the organization of the police department of this city . . .
> This conclusion is not reached by snap judgement, but after long and careful consideration . . . I long ago reached the conclusion that the Los Angeles Police Department Union must go. The only reason for my hesitancy in taking action was the fact that during its entire history it has made petty and scurrilous attacks on me and the Chief of Police and I did not want it to appear that any official act of mine would be in the nature of retaliation. However, the police union has itself brought the matter squarely before me by insisting upon payroll deductions of members of the union and that such deductions be provided for by ordinance . . .
>
> For the information of the Council, I state that I will present to the Police Commission at its next regular meeting a recommendation that it adopt a regulation under the rule making power of the department, providing that no police officer may be a member of a labor union.

To bring an end to these activities, the Los Angeles Board of Police Commissioners adopted a resolution on March 12, 1946, providing, among other things, that:

> No police officer of the Los Angeles Police Department shall hereafter be or become a member of any police officers' organization in any manner identified with any trade association, federation of labor union which admits to membership persons who are not members of the Los Angeles Police Department, or whose membership is not exclusively made up of employees of the City of Los Angeles.

One of the police officers, a member of the union, attacked the resolution in a court proceeding. The court sustained the action of the Police Commission, and the case was appealed to the District Court of Appeals. In March 1947, the District Court of Appeals upheld the lower court and sustained the validity of the resolution adopted by the Board of Police Commissioners.

[41]*Ibid.*, p. 291.

Again, in October 1949, the California Appellate Court considered the problem in a case involving an attempt to strike and picket the Department of Water and Power of the City of Los Angeles. There the court said, after reviewing all of the earlier cases:

> The controlling principle of the foregoing cases is that employment in the public service frequently entails a necessary surrender of civil rights to a limited extent because of the dominant public interest in the unimpeded and uninterrupted performance of the functions of government. Fair treatment for public employees does not require legal protection for concerted labor action generally, as in the case of private employment, compelled to a considerable extent by law.

Despite these previous reverses, during 1945, the AFSCME chartered a police union in St. Louis, Missouri. Like the Boston police, this department is governed by a Board of Police Commissioners appointed by the governor. After the Boston strike, the St. Louis Board adopted a regulation forbidding police membership in "any association, meeting, union, or any organization of members or employees other than the Police Relief Association, the Police Funeral Association, and the St. Louis Pension Fund Association." Later, when the union was formed, the governor issued a statement declaring, "History reveals the dangers inherent in the organizing of peace officers into unions." Shortly afterwards, the president and treasurer of the union were tried, found guilty, and ordered dismissed from the service for violation of the departmental rules. After a court appeal failed, the Police Board issued an order declaring that any of the nearly 600 members of the union who failed to withdraw would be discharged. All but five members (these were later removed) obeyed the order. The union then severed its affiliation with the labor movement and reconstituted itself into an independent organization, called the Shield Club, which the department recognized.[42]

Early in 1946, a similar situation arose in Wichita, Kansas, when the city council declared that "no recognition of any kind would be given to a police union." Seven officers of the union were discharged. The state court denied a "writ of mandamus"

---

[42]*Ibid.*, pp. 291-292.

to compel the city manager to reinstate them. At the same time, the city council adopted a resolution stating the conditions under which it would recognize a purely local organization of police. The union gradually succumbed to the pressure.[43]

However, it was in Jackson, Mississippi, that the most thorough-going attempt to challenge the restrictions against police union-ization was made. Thirty-six members of a police local were dismissed by the city commission in 1946. The men appealed to the circuit court and were given a jury trial. At the trial, the city made the usual contention that union membership meant divided allegiance, thus, a threat to public authority. The jury returned a unanimous verdict in favor of the union. Subsequent-ly, the state supreme court reversed the verdict, upholding the right of the city to discharge the policemen for union member-ship.[44] The Supreme Court of the United States refused to re-view the case.[45]

Despite the opposition that the AFSCME faced, its police locals grew to 55 by 1947; after a recession over the next few years, it reached 61 by 1951, but had fallen to 58 in 1953.[46]

Reports incicate, however, that these AFSCME locals were transitory in nature. According to a survey made by the Louis-ville Police Department in 1957, questionnaires were sent to 55 cities who reported police unions in 1944. Forty-four of the cities replied. Within twelve years, 28 unions (64% of the total reply-ing) were no longer in existence; only 16 cities continued their union membership, four of which were small in number and considered inactive; one was associated with a police benefit and protective association. Thus, only 11 police departments of the original 44 had unions at that time.[47]

By 1959, AFSCME had, however, organized 65 locals[48] and in October of 1966, the President of AFSCME stated, "We do have police unions including about 10,000 policemen in 65 locals

[43]*Ibid.*, p. 292.

[44]*Ibid.*, pp. 292-293.

[45]*City of Jackson v. McLoed* (1946) 24 So. (2d) 319; 90 L. Ed. 1261.

[46]Audrey M. Davies: History and legality of police unions. *GRA Reporter*, Vol. 5, July-August 1953, p. 42.

[47]Carl E. Heustis, *op. cit.*, p. 644.

[48]M. W. Aussieker, Jr., *op. cit.*, p. 11.

in our organization."[49] Conversely, a *Fortune* survey in 1968 placed the AFSCME police strength at 7,000 in 58 locals.[50] Since Local 1195 of the Baltimore Police was chartered in April 1966, AFSCME has failed to win a contested representation election involving the police.[51] The New York State Troopers spurned AFSCME in favor of the Patrolmen's Benevolent Association in 1969.[52]

Yet, in December of 1970, AFSCME claimed to represent approximately 11,000 policemen and sheriff's department employees. Ten thousand of these were in some 90 local police unions in 20 states. The remaining 1,000 policemen held membership in 36 locals in 15 states; each local represents police along with other public employees.[53] These statistics represent a membership growth of 10 percent in one year and an approximate 38 percent total increase in local police unions. Membership appears to center in Colorado, Connecticut, Illinois, Maryland, Massachusetts, Michigan, Minnesota, Nebraska, New York, Oregon, Tennessee, and Wisconsin.[54] A typical AFSCME police contract (between Multnomah County, Oregon, and Multnomah County Police Union Local 117) is included as Appendix B.

Over the years, various AFSCME police locals successfully negotiated contracts for their members without resorting to the use of the strike (this was prior to the 1970 removal of the strike restrictions—see Appendix A). Fortunately, they accomplished their purpose by undertaking public relations campaigns to gain public support. For example, in 1966, the Omaha AFSCME local gained a 15 percent pay increase after the results of a wage survey were published in local newspapers.[55] In Bridgeport, Connecticut (1967), police received a $920 annual raise, bringing their salaries from the lowest to the highest in the state. Again,

49Jerry Wurf: Coming unionized government. *Public Employee.* October 1966.

50M. W. Aussieker, Jr., *op. cit.,* p. 11.

51Baltimore police union chartered. *Public Employee,* April 1966, p. 4.

52PBA wins state trooper run-off election. *New York Times,* August 31, 1969, p. 25.

53Private communication with Mr. D. S. Wasserman, Director, Department of Research, AFSCME, December 2, 1970.

54*Ibid.*

55Omaha police get 15% pay increases. *Public Employee,* November 1966, p. 5.

the success of negotiations was attributed to a public relations campaign.[56] Similarly, public relations campaigns were later undertaken by the police locals in West Hartford, Connecticut and Auburn, New York, resulting in $400 to $500 annual wage increases.[57]

INTERNATIONAL BROTHERHOOD OF TEAMSTERS, CHAUFFERS, WAREHOUSEMEN AND HELPERS UNION

In addition to AFSCME activity, several affiliated AFL-CIO and unaffiliated trade unions appear to be interested in organizing the police. The most aggressive of these has been the International Brotherhood of Teamsters, Chauffeurs, Warehousemen and Helpers Union. In 1958, under the leadership of its president, James Hoffa, the union announced plans to organize all police in the nation. As a result, a dozen bills were introduced in various state legislatures prohibiting these Teamster-sponsored police unions, and a legislative investigation of the Teamsters was considered by several Congressional leaders.[58] In fact, adverse reaction to Teamsters' plans was so severe that on January 1, 1959, Mr. Hoffa announced that he was sorry that he had ever started the national drive to organize the police.[59]

On the other hand and despite the bad beginning, the Teamsters have been able to organize several police departments throughout the country. Most of the Teamsters locals are in small cities—Ansonia and Shellia, in Connecticut, and Escanaba, Michigan. Additionally, 110 out of 186 employees in the San Francisco Sheriff's Office have joined the Teamsters, who represents them before the Board of Supervisors. "The deputies have gained wage increases and are eligible to participate in the Teamsters' health and welfare programs."[60] It is interesting to note, however, that the Teamster charter for police locals specifies that

[56]Connecticut police local gains a $920 increase. *Public Employee*, March 1967, p. 10.

[57]M. W. Aussieker, Jr., *op. cit.*, pp. 11-12.

[58]*Ibid.*, p. 13.

[59]A. H. Raskin: Hoffa regrets police union attempt. *New York Times*, January 1, 1959, p. 1.

[60]Now policemen are joining the teamsters. *U. S. News and World Report*, January 16, 1967, p. 8.

the document will be revoked if policemen, "strike or refuse in concert to perform their duties."[61]

Clearly, Teamster interest is increasing. In September of 1970, the general vice president of the union issued a bulletin to all area directors, general organizers, joint councils, and local unions urging that they develop an organizing campaign among public employees at all levels of government (see Appendix D for a copy of this bulletin). At the same time, the Teamsters claimed to represent 2,349 policemen (see Table 2 of Appendix D) in a number of departments scattered across the county.

SERVICE EMPLOYEES UNION

In addition to the Teamsters a few police locals have been established in the Service Employees International Union, which also forbids policemen from striking. In fact, the Teamsters and the Service Employees are the only nonpublic employee labor unions to organize police into locals, but several other trade unions have accepted police associations as affiliates. For example, the Police Association of Alameda, California, affiliated with Carpenters Local 261 in 1968. Under the arrangement, the Carpenters' Local business agent represents the police in their economic bargaining with the City of Alameda, but an Alameda Police Association continues to serve as the official spokesman for the police in other matters. Grievances, for example, are handled by the president of the Association, which continues to provide recreational, social, and benevolent activities for its members.[62]

Considering public antagonism toward both the Teamsters and the Transport Workers' Unions (another service employee union which has made gestures in the direction of organizing policemen), these organizations will in the future likely be restricted to assisting police benevolent associations in obtaining representation rights. An example is found in the reaction after the Teamsters announced they had plans to organize the New

[61]Joseph Lowenberg: Labor relations for policemen and firefighters. *Monthly Labor Review*, Vol. 91, May 1968, p. 36.
[62]M. W. Aussieker, Jr., *op. cit.*, p. 13.

York City Patrolmen's Benevolent Association as the official bargaining representative for New York City patrolmen.[63]

FRATERNAL ORDER OF POLICE

In addition to the Teamsters, AFL-CIO affiliated locals, the Service Employees International Union, and the American Federation of State, County and Municipal Employees, the Fraternal Order of Police, founded in 1915, is currently reported to maintain some 900 locals with a total membership of 90,000 policemen (a highly controversial figure). Its president is the only full-time member of the staff. The FOP, in contrast to AFSCME, is not affiliated with the AFL-CIO and does not consider itself a labor union. It appears to be a loose confederation of low-dues local lodges with the national encouraging autonomy for these local units.

The autonomy of FOP lodges can best be illustrated by their collective bargaining activities. Although the national and state FOP associations contend that they are opposed to strikes, three FOP locals have engaged in concerted jobs actions. In September 1967, 90 percent of the FOP policemen and firemen of Youngstown, Ohio, refused to report to work. The dispute arose over police demands for a $1,200 annual salary increase. In fact, they did not return to work until the city obtained an injunction. However, a permanent injunction was provided only after the Common Pleas Judge obtained agreement from the city that it would grant pay raises to the policemen and firemen. The settlement offer was a $100-a-month salary increase for both.[64]

Similarly in 1968, FOP locals in Pontiac, Michigan, and Salem, Ohio, engaged in concerted job activities to support their demands for higher wages. In both cases, the police eventually were successful in obtaining their original demands almost intact. Moreover, a more conventional approach to obtaining wage increases was utilized by the Cleveland lodge of the FOP. They accomplished "potent politicking" and picketed city hall which resulted in a successful referendum that granted policemen large pay raises.[65]

[63]*Ibid.*
[64]*New York Times*, September 8, 1967, p. 1.
[65]Labor letter. *Wall Street Journal*, November 16, 1968, p. 1.

Newark, New Jersey policemen are unique in that they hold membership in both the local Patrolmen's Benevolent Association and the FOP. The PBA president and a 100-man executive board recently conducted negotiations with the city regarding wages and fringe benefits. In 1968, the executive board recommended "strict enforcement of the law" by Newark police to remind the business community of the serious crisis in police salaries.[66] While the PBA in Newark has focused on bargaining, the FOP has represented the police in the courts, attempting to enjoin the city from forcing police to work overtime without compensation.[67] The Newark FOP lodge has been equally active politically. Regarding the "Kerner Report's" findings on the causes of the Newark riots, an FOP spokesman said, "We are bending once more to the demands of civil rights groups. . . . The inevitable feeling that the Newark police were the cause of the disorder pervaded the entire document."[68]

In the near future the FOP may come to play the same role in other areas as it has in Newark because this organization tends to regard itself as a professional association rather than as a labor union. Its attitude is based primarily upon the fact that the organization has several national and state committees which formulate position papers on various aspects of police work (i.e. Committee on Human Rights and Law Enforcement has published three reports regarding Civilian Review Boards). On the other hand, the courts and administrative agencies appear to disagree regarding its status. For example, the Rhode Island State Labor Relations Board ruled in 1963 that the FOP was a lodge and consequently could not represent the police.[69] However, in 1965, the Delaware Director of Public Safety ordered 180 policemen, who joined the FOP, to resign at once and not to associate directly or indirectly with the parent organization; "members of the police department in any city do not have the right to join

---

[66]Newark police begin strict enforcement of the law. *New York Times,* October 21, 1968, p. 1.

[67]Newark FOP challenges overtime rule. *New York Times,* June 6, 1965, p. 74.

[68]FOP scores Kerner Report. *New York Times,* February 14, 1968, p. 1.

[69]*New York Times,* July 11, 1963, p. 12.

a labor union."[70] Authorities in Detroit have also banned the FOP on the ground that its stimulation of activity in the field of pensions, salaries, and general police legislation tended to undermine the discipline of the force.[71]

POLICY OF NONAFFILIATED ASSOCIATIONS

When the AFL-CIO sanctioned the concept of a national police union in 1969, the Boston Police Patrolmen's Benevolent Association and the Detroit Police Officers' Association sent letters to police groups in 100 cities opposing ties with organized labor. This opposition, which seems to reflect the policy of most nonaffiliated police associations, was based on two principles: (1) the AFL-CIO union had refused to approve the police right to strike (now obsolete because of the change in AFSCME), and (2) national affiliation reduces the local association's effectiveness in community politics.[72]

The rationale regarding the first principle is that no national affiliation means the right-to-strike issue is determined by local associations. Yet, past experiences with nonaffiliated associations in Detroit and New York indicate little hesitancy in applying this or similar tactics. The Detroit association initiated a "sick-in" during 1967 negotiations which resulted in the policemen obtaining a $10,000 maximum annual salary, the highest in the nation at the time.[73] New York City's Policemen's Benevolent Association called slowdowns and sick-ins during negotiations in 1962, 1966, and 1968.

Yet, the effectiveness of the New York PBA in obtaining economic benefits for its members seems confusing. In the Keyserling survey of police salaries in 1960, the New York City Police were the fourth highest paid in the United States.[74] In 1969, New York police salaries ranked ninth among cities with populations over 500,000, but a *New York Times* survey in 1967 found

[70]Wilmington, Delaware police barred from FOP membership. *New York Times,* September 12, 1965, p. 129.

[71]Sterling D. Spero, *op. cit.,* p. 293.

[72]Labor letter. *Wall Street Journal,* February 18, 1969, p. 1.

[73]Detroit policemen get raise. *New York Times,* February 28, 1967, p. 37.

[74]Leon H. Keyserling police salary survey. *New York Times,* March 22, 1960, p. 39.

that, including fringe benefits in total compensation, the New York City policemen were the highest paid in the United States.[75]

In any event, the independent associations are most effective in their pursuit of the second principle—political activities. Police membership in the John Birch Society attracted national attention after Boston patrolmen supported an ultraconservative candidate during the 1964 Boston Mayoralty race. The New York City Patrolmen's Benevolent Association's greatest political victory was accomplished in its fight through the courts and at the polls against a proposed Civilian Review Board. On the state level in 1956, the PBA was able to lobby potently for a maximum 40-hour work-week for police and for a state law (in 1960) permitting policemen and firemen to "moonlight."[76]

Conversely, the New York City PBA has clearly proven itself to be highly autocratic. "The PBA lacks a democratic base; leadership is executive-dominated by a few high ranking personnel with special interests."[77] In the 1968 negotiations, bargaining was conducted entirely by PBA President John J. Casseese and his public relations assistant—possibly accounting for the rejection of the contract by the general membership.[78]

This rejection of the 1968 contract and the consequent formation of a new 35-man bargaining team illustrates the brewing discontent of the more militant members in the New York organization. The Civilian Review Board question was another issue that caused discontent in the PBA; a 5,000 man group within the organization recently filed suit to prevent the use of dues to campaign against the Review Board. Clearly, pluralism is increasing within the PBA.

However, it is the many nonaffiliated associations (like the PBA, that face the least resistance from public officials in organizing policemen. When the Transport Workers' Union (AFL-CIO) announced an intention to organize New York Policemen, Rule 225 of the Police Department Rules and Regulations was amended to read, "No member of the police force of the City

---

[75]Detroit policemen get raises. *New York Times*, February 28, 1967, p. 37.
[76]M. W. Aussieker, Jr., *op. cit.*, p. 15.
[77]Edmund P. Murray: Should police unionize. *The Nation*, June 13, 1959, p. 533.
[78]Why policemen are unhappy. *New York Times*, October 24, 1968, p. 59.

of New York shall become a member of a labor union."[79] Yet, New York City policemen are able to maintain their membership in the PBA, which has the following purpose, according to its constitution:[80]

> To act as a bargaining agent on behalf of all the Patrolmen of the police force of the City of New York in matters of policy, salaries, hours of employment and all other matters relating to the general welfare of the members thereof.

A PROPOSED AFL-CIO POLICE UNION

In February of 1969, the New York PBA asked for affiliation with the AFL-CIO; the latter formed a special committee to study the feasibility of an AFL-CIO national police union. On February 21, 1969, this special committee authorized President George Meany to issue a charter for a policemen's union if and when: (1) a suitable consitutional structure has been drawn up, on a national basis, "with commitments of affiliation of police organizations in a representative number of cities"; and (2) "satisfactory assurances are received that such an organization will confine itself strictly to its jurisdiction and will not encroach upon areas of employment represented by existing AFL-CIO affiliation."[81]

Commenting on the authorization, Norman Frank of the New York PBA said, "As far as we are concerned, the council's action represents the beginning . . . Chicago, Kansas City, and San Francisco police are interested in joining us."[82] John Casseese, then President of the PBA, said, "the new organization would confine itself to its intended jurisdiction over state, county, and local police."[83] A suitable constitution has been interpreted by George Meany to include a no-strike clause in the union charter.[84]

The constitution of the first proposed national police union has been written (completed in Omaha, Nebraska, on November

[79]New York City Department of Labor, *Report on the Recognition and Organization of Unionized Police,* New York City, 1958, p. 3.

[80]*Ibid.*

[81]Police union authorized. *AFL-CIO News,* February 22, 1969, p. 1.

[82]AFL-CIO Police Union. *Newsweek,* March 3, 1969, p. 73.

[83]*Ibid.*

[84]AFL-CIO charters a police union. *San Francisco Chronicle,* February 21, 1969, p. 2.

2, 1969) by a committee of 30 policemen from New York and 11 other cities. It also contains a no-strike clause. The chairman of the drafting committee was John J. Casseese, former President of the New York PBA.[85]

The proposed new organization would be known as the International Brotherhood of Police Officers; and, according to many police experts, is a strong manifestation of a wave of militancy that has swept through many American police departments in the past few years. Mr. Casseese has said the purpose of the proposed union is to unite all American policemen into a single organization and win for them improved wages, hours, and working conditions. Currently, American police consists of 40,000 separate police agencies in the United States, employing over 400,000 policemen[86]—a powerful force to be reckoned with in the event of success in national unionization.

Without doubt one purpose of the proposed union is also to give policemen a voice in Washington. One delegate has said:[87]

Right now we're organized in Salt Lake, so if the mayor does not do what we want him to do, we defeat him at the polls. And someday we'll have that nationally.

In the closed meeting in Omaha, the cities represented included New York; Chicago; Portland, Oregon; Kansas City; Salt Lake City; St. Paul; San Jose, California; Auburn, New York; Quincy, Massachusetts; Shreveport, Louisiana; and New Britain, Connecticut.[88-89]

[85]Police bar strikes in proposed union. *New York Times,* November 3, 1969.
[86]*Ibid.*
[87]*Ibid.*
[88]*Ibid.*
[89]At the mid-winter 1971 meeting of the AFL-CIO Executive Council, the International Brotherhood of Police Officers was turned down in their request for a charter because they are still largely a paper organization. (Personal correspondence with Mr. D. S. Wasserman, Director, Department of Research, AFSCME, March 1971.)

Chapter IV

THE CALIFORNIA SCENE

California proved almost as difficult, in the matter of obtaining data on the part of these researchers, as the more remote locations of the country. Here, as elsewhere, union officials, public officials, and policemen were reluctant to discuss the issue of "police unionization."

Most policemen who were interviewed indicated that they were highly satisfied with confining their representation to their local associations, possibly with some statewide ties; but, very few expressed a desire to affiliate with organized labor. However, the majority also expressed a desire for collective bargaining. It appears that the "issues" in California are identical to those in other sections of the country: wages, conditions of work, increased dangers of the job, status-prestige, grievance procedures, and benefits. The approaches to solving these problems also are the same: sick-ins, sick-outs, slowdowns, strict enforcement, and the strike. Affiliations are similar: the statewide and local associations as well as membership in labor unions. In California, however, another association, somewhat reminiscent of the Fraternal Order of Police, is highly active on the scene—PORAC, the Peace Officers Research Association of California. This organization also proved similar to the FOP in that its officials ignored these researchers' inquiries and were not available for discussion.

Eleven law enforcement associations exist in the state. These ars as follows:[1]

1. California Peace Officers Association
2. Police Chiefs' Division, League of California Cities
3. California State Sheriffs' Association

[1]*Journal of California Law Enforcement,* Vol. 5, No. 2, California Peace Officers' Association, Sacramento, California, October 1970, p. 104.

4. California State Division, International Association of Identication
5. California Police Chiefs' Association
6. California Check Investigators' Association
7. Southern California Association of Fingerprint Officers
8. FBI National Academy Associates, California Chapter
9. California State Juvenile Officers' Association
10. Women Peace Officers' Association of California
11. Peace Officers Research Association of California

Of this grouping, it is the last one, PORAC, that is particularly significant in context with police unionization; this organization will subsequently be discussed in detail, along with California's first and second police strikes in Vallejo and Antioch, respectively.

As of July 1, 1969, 402 cities had been incorporated within the state. Of these, 62 were contracting for police services with existing law enforcement agencies. The remaining 340 maintained their own enforcement agencies.[2] The state also had 58 Sheriff's departments, 18 Marshal's offices,[3] a State Highway Patrol, and a State Police. One hundred eighty-six police departments, 33 Sheriff's departments, 15 Marshal's offices,[4] the Highway Patrol, and the State Police now have their own membership organizations. In 1968, PORAC claimed that 140 of the municipal, 16 Sheriff's and 12 Marshal's associations were affiliated with it.[5]

California also has a provision in its Government Code, commonly referred to as the Meyers-Milias-Brown Act of 1968, which states a purpose to promote the following:

> full communication between public employers and their employees by providing a reasonable method of resolving disputes regarding wages, hours, and other terms and conditions of employment between public employers and public employee organizations.

---

[2] *1969-1970 Annual Salary Survey,* Peace Officers Research Association of California, October 28, 1969, p. ii.

[3] *Ibid.,* pp. 31-32.

[4] *Ibid.,* pp. 61-88.

[5] *1968-1969 Annual Salary Survey,* Peace Officers Research Association of California, October 30, 1968, pp. 49-71.

In effect, it only requires government bodies to meet with public workers (see Appendix E for the full text of the act). Thus, California appears to recognize the collective bargaining rights of public employees while a number of unresolved conflicts and "loopholes" exist in the act. Public employees remain unhappy with the provisions of the bill, and even its coauthors have admitted its inadequacies. The net result is a muddled relationship between employee groups and the public employers.

Additionally, the Meyers-Milias-Brown Act appears to have done little to advance the collective bargaining concept when expressed as a police objective. By the end of 1969 only 20 California cities had adopted ordinances granting employee salary negotiation privileges.[6] Negotiations by police representatives were successful in San Jose, Alameda County, Santa Clara County, and Torrance.[7]

In December 1970, the Attorney General of the state of California rendered his opinion that public employees do not have the right to strike—also that police and firemen from other areas may be called into a city where local police or firemen are on strike.[8]

The increasing militancy of California policemen, implementation of police strike action, and the confusion of existing law recently resulted in the introduction of a bill ("Dills"—SB No. 333)[9] requiring compulsory arbitration to settle labor disputes involving fire fighters and law enforcement officers. The text of this bill is included as Appendix F.

The Dills Bill continues the public employee prohibition against strikes. Where local governing bodies cannot resolve salary disputes or experience impasses, compulsory final and binding arbitration will take place. This precludes strikes, slowdowns, sick-outs, and other detrimental job actions.[10] The bill is currently undergoing interim committee study, but the concept itself

[6]Policemen in state considering unions. *San Diego Evening Tribune,* October 29, 1969.

[7]Police adopt policy for pay, benefits. *San Diego Evening Tribune,* November 1, 1969.

[8]New Ruling on police fire strikes. *The Sacramento Union,* December 30, 1970.

[9]Bill calls for settlement of firemen, police strikes by compulsory arbitration. *Sacramento Bee,* February 18, 1971.

[10]*Ibid.*

has been the subject of opposition by many public administrators who think that the third party will fail to represent the citizens of the community as adequately as its public officials.

PEACE OFFICERS RESEARCH ASSOCIATION OF CALIFORNIA (PORAC)

In addition to recent labor law and proposed legislation in the Dills Bill, the most significant development in the police union area has been the combined activities of PORAC.

The objectives of the Peace Officers Research Association of California, as stated in Article II of its constitution, are as follows:

> The object and purpose of the Association shall be to collect, study, standardize, summarize, and to disseminate factual data for the purpose of promoting the professionalization of the police service, and to stimulate mutual cooperation between law enforcement agencies.

For eighteen years, since 1951, PORAC remained a little known organization, researching comparative salary information. In November 1969, at San Diego, it was transformed into a full-blown bargaining agency for California law enforcement officers.[11]

Representatives of police departments throughout the state redrafted the organization's bylaws and decided to put more money into an effort to provide the "muscle" necessary to deal with city and county governments.[12]

Oakland officers spearheaded this reorganization with the support of policemen from San Francisco, Los Angeles, San Diego, San Jose, and Vallejo.[13]

PORAC announced plans to establish headquarters in Sacramento with both a full-time executive secretary and a legislative advocate. To pay for this, individual membership dues were raised from one to 12 dollars annually. Membership at that time was between 20,000 and 25,000 from local affiliated organizations who offered a potential of 30,000 to 35,000 policemen and sheriff's

[11]New punch in police bargaining. *Oakland Tribune*, November 9, 1969, p. 1.
[12]*Ibid.*
[13]*Ibid.*
[14]*Ibid.*

deputies in the state.[14] For organizational purposes, the state was divided by PORAC into four zones with three chapters in each.[15]

This move toward strengthening the organization was made while representatives of police departments from 14 American cities were forming the International Brotherhood of Police Officers in Omaha, Nebraska. According to organizational spokesmen, the buildup of PORAC stemmed from the police strike in Vallejo.[16] PORAC's new bylaws were silent on the subject of strikes as a means of enforcing demands.[17]

The question of whether policemen or other public employees in California have the right to strike still has not been settled in the courts. Vallejo policemen and firemen defied a court order during their July 17 to July 22, 1969 strike; this strike was settled before the scheduled court hearing. Oakland policemen had been on the verge of striking for higher pay and benefits before the Vallejo one.[18]

Perhaps the new militancy adopted by PORAC as well as an insight into its future attitudes is best revealed by a motion passed unanimously at the PORAC Executive Board meeting on October 27, 1970 at the Sahara Tahoe Hotel in Stateline, Nevada:

MOVED that the Board of Directors, during the year 1971, establish pilot regional negotiating areas of selected parts of the State. That within these areas, the chapters and zone involved, in cooperation with the Board of Directors and with its approval, establish certain minimum standards of wages, hours and other such conditions of employment as may appear proper to be demanded from the employing entities within the regional area selected. That following the adoption of these standards, it be agreed that no association within such region will settle with its employer until all of the public entities involved be agreed to provide to all of the associations involved such minimum standards.

PORAC was flexing its muscles as an aftermath of its success in the Vallejo police strike of 1969.

[15]*Ibid.*
[16]*Ibid.*, p. 6.
[17]*Ibid.*
[18]*Ibid.*

THE VALLEJO POLICE STRIKE

Policemen in Vallejo, California (population: 70,000), entered into a joint effort with the fire fighters of that city in the spring and summer of 1969 seeking higher wages and improved fringe benefits. The city council held out for a flat wage increase of 5 percent. When the involved associations and the city reached an impasse, 90 policemen and 88 fire fighters went out on strike (July 17, 1969) and didn't return to work until July 22nd. This gave California its first joint police/firemen's strike and its first police strike.

The issues for the policemen involved the following:
1. A 5% pay increase over that offered by the city.
2. Time and one-half compensation for overtime or equal time off.
3. Callback pay at a minimum of four hours.
4. Home standby at straight time pay.
5. Longevity pay for career personnel based upon 2½% for each five years, up to 20 years of service.
6. A retirement system based upon that of the California State Highway Patrol.
7. An increased educational incentive pay program (7½% for intermediate or advanced college certificates).

While the city manager enunciated agreement with the bulk of these demands, the council rejected all of them. Therefore, the attorney for the two associations, who also was the attorney for PORAC, advised the police and firemen that their individual citizen's prerogatives were to picket, boycott, and strike.

A strike vote was taken on July 16th, and full backing of the membership was accorded the executive boards of the two associations. Announcement of the strike for the following morning was made. Pickets would be posted at the police station, fire department headquarters, the new library site, city hall, and the corporation yards. Additionally, the Solano County Central Labor Council gave sanction to the action and so advised city hall.[19]

Last minute counteroffers and negotiations broke down, and the city manager branded the impending walkout as an "unlawful

[19]Uniformed groups won't report for shifts in morning. *Vallejo Times-Herald,* July 16, 1969, p. 1.

strike." He indicated a restraining order would be obtained and assistance sought from the Solano County Sheriff's Department.[20] The walkout took place as scheduled, in defiance of a Superior Court restraining order.[21] City officials immediately asked for state aid while the strikers posted pickets as announced, as well as at the fire substations. One hundred building trades employees honored the picket line. Again branding the strike as "unlawful," the city manager threatened disciplinary action against all involved. Both sides viewed the strike as a "test case," under the watchful eye of the entire state.[22]

The Solano County Sheriff's Department sent units to assist in operating a skeletal force, which was now composed of the chief, two subordinates, and other city managerial personnel. State aid was again requested. However, no declaration of a state of emergency was legally possible in a labor dispute, and some state delaying tactics were encountered.[23] During this time, the pickets marched in defiance of the court order and distributed leaflets soliciting public support for their cause.

On July 18, Governor Reagan branded the strike as "extremely unforunate" and "illegal." He promised state assistance to protect public safety in response to appeals from city officials. The governor said:[24]

> Protection of life and property must be guaranteed. As Governor, I will not permit any citizen of California at any time to be denied vital police and fire protection services. The state will meet this situation which now exists in Vallejo with whatever assistance it can and should provide. No one has the right to strike against the public safety. I want to assure the citizens of Vallejo that their right to police and fire protection will be met, and I have communicated that assurance to local officials. That same assurance also is given to all citizens of California.

Units of the California Highway Patrol were made available

---

[20]Vallejo to seek court restraining order on walkout. *Vallejo Times-Herald,* July 17, 1969, p. 1.

[21]Police, firemen strike; court injunction ignored. *Vallejo News Chronicle,* July 17, 1969.

[22]*Ibid.*

[23]*Ibid.*

[24]Public protection will be provided. *Vallejo News Chronicle,* July 18, 1969, p. 1.

for emergency service in Vallejo, along with state fire fighting equipment and personnel.[25] Fortunately, no major crimes or fires occurred.

Picketing continued and building trades workers still refused to cross the picket line, shutting down some four million dollars in projects. Additionally, policemen and firemen from other cities appeared in Vallejo and joined the picket lines. Meanwhile, the counsel for the associations met with a city councilman to discuss the possibility of third party arbitration.[26]

On the fourth day of the strike, July 20, the associations decided to appeal to the public and announced a rally scheduled for July 21. They also threatened legal action to limit the powers of the governor to interfere and asked for a meeting or negotiating session with the city council. During this time, the manning provided by the California Highway Patrol and the Solano County Sheriff's Department was comparable to that normally available. The California Highway Patrol had assigned 24 traffic officers, three sergeants, one lieutenant, and a captain.[27] All of these state-provided police and fire services were, however, reimbursable by contract.

In its July 21 edition, the *Vallejo News Chronicle* took this editorial stand in connection with the strike:[28]

The strike action taken last Wednesday by the rank and file of Vallejo's police and fire departments is regrettable. It reflects a perverse attitude on the part of our public safety employees to place their own ends above the security of the community to which they have taken an oath to safeguard.

Vallejo's uniform personnel went on strike because the City Council, who had already granted them a five per cent pay boost under the 1969-1970 municipal budget, refused to accede to their demands for another five per cent salary increase as well as additional benefits or to submit the dispute to mediation. We believe the City Council responded reasonably in its final offer made Sunday night to submit to non-binding

[25]*Ibid.*

[26]Another executive council meeting on strike tonight. *Vallejo News Chronicle,* July 18, 1969, p. 1.

[27]Two unions slate outdoor meeting for Monday night. *Vallejo Times-Herald,* July 20, 1969, p. 1.

[28]City council has made fair offer. *Vallejo News Chronicle,* July 21, 1969, p. 1.

negotiations or to grant seven per cent pay increases to both firemen and police officers, in addition to a shorter work week for fire fighters, and other concessions. It is our opinion that the City Council has gone far enough in acceding to the demands of the strikers and that it now is time for our public safety employees to act reasonably by accepting the Council's compromise offer and returning to work. Their responsibility to the community in their sworn duty to maintain law and order and to protect life and property now transcends all other considerations.

The strikers have been given a fair offer made in open session and thus, in effect, publicly debated as the police and firemen have demanded. We congratulate the City Council on its stand and fully support its position in seeking to resolve realistically a situation that already has prevailed too long and which might have been averted had the strikers sought counsel more locally indoctrinated who could have weighted the demands against the welfare of the community rather than directed solely towards their own objectives. In this respect, it is our belief that the dispute should never have involved the police and firemen together. We feel the nature of their duties make firemen and policemen separate elements of public safety and they, therefore, should be treated separately. There is a distinct difference between law enforcement and fire suppression. A difference which should never permit police officers to go on strike.

Officers who accept the responsibility of law enforcement should be compensated adequately for their services within the city's ability to pay for them, but the right for them to strike at the peril of the community they are sworn to protect is an abrogation of their obligations which never should be permitted.

Vallejo's strike of public safety employees now is in its fifth day, the issues have been debated, and equitable compromise has been offered. It is time for reason to prevail. It is time to put an end to this dispute, to get to the job of restoring peace and harmony, law and order, and the protection of life and property. It is time to begin rebuilding Vallejo's damaged image in a spirit of cooperation and mutual respect; in short, it is time to go back to work!

The first hopeful sign for a break in the strike appeared on the fifth day when the city council made two offers that were summarily rejected by the associations' counsel; however, this still caused optimism for a reopening of further negotiations. This also was the day for a public meeting where the strikers attempted to explain their positions to the public. California Highway Patrol and Solano County deputies continued to patrol the city while State Division of Forestry crews manned the city's six fire stations.[29]

The five-day strike was settled at a regular meeting of the city council in the evening of July 21, 1969, with the strikers scheduled to return to duty on the morning of July 22. The settlement was based upon a compromise package as well as assurances of amnesty for the strikers and no loss of paycheck dollars for the strike period. The police package provided the following:[30]

1. A 2% pay increase over the 5% previously granted (this changed the starting pay scale from $630 per month to $706 per month or—with three years longevity—from $841 to $857).
2. A choice between straight time pay for overtime or time and one-half for such overtime if taken as compensatory time (the time off provision was good only if operations permit).
3. The educational pay incentive was increased from $2\frac{1}{2}$% of salary to 5% for those holding Associate of Arts degrees or intermediate POST (Peace Officers Standards and Training) certificates. For those with Bachelor of Arts degrees or advanced POST certificates, this percentage increased from 5% to $7\frac{1}{2}$%.

To avoid any loss in paychecks for the strike period, the strikers forfeited equivalent accrued overtime or annual leave. This agreement was reached over the protests of the mayor, who did not want to pay the strikers for the time they were off duty.[31] Additionally, Vallejo withdrew its complaint from the court, thereby avoiding a judicial test of the situation.

Neither side could claim a "cleancut" victory in this "test" case. All of the strikers' announced goals were not achieved, and the city "backed down" from its original position.[32] A significant fact is that public safety employees struck in violation of California law, and no penalty test was ever undertaken in the courts by the state.

During the strike, estimates were that outside state assistance

[29]Hopeful sign in strike. *Vallejo News Chronicle*, July 21, 1969, p. 1.
[30]Police, fire walkout ends. *Vallejo Times-Herald*, July 21, 1969, p. 1.
[31]*Ibid.*
[32]Extra effort helps avert city crisis. *Vallejo Times-Herald*, July 27, 1969, p. 1.

costs would range between $20,000 and $40,000. Actual costs amounted to $17,802.[33]

THE ANTIOCH POLICE STRIKE

On July 11, 1970, the Antioch police took its cue from Vallejo, thus initiating the second police strike in the history of the state. The facts were that in early summer of 1970, the Antioch Police Association and the City of Antioch (population: 26,000) entered into preliminary discussions regarding a salary increase for the police. The city offered 7½ percent while the policemen demanded 16 percent. A counteroffer of eight percent then was made by the city manager, providing that the police met the following conditions:[34]

> The Antioch Police Association shall reaffirm their pledge to our community not to engage or support any concerted employee action such as a strike, walk-out, sick-in, sick-out, blue-out, brown-out, or any similar tactic.
> 2. The Antioch Police Association shall actively support action to have PORAC to withdraw and discontinue all legislative activities at the state and federal levels . . .

The Antioch Police Association then turned to PORAC, asking its assistance. This was forthcoming in the form of the PORAC attorney, who contended that the city manager's offer violated the constitutional rights of the policemen under the First Amendment. Also, that it was in violation of the state labor code and would deprive police officers of their civil rights.[35]

On July 2, 1970, Antioch policemen attempted to contact the city manager for further discussions, but found him unavailable. They then announced that the following alternatives were open to them:[36]

1. No raise whatsoever.
2. Accept a 7½% raise without "strings."
3. Give up PORAC and receive an 8% raise.
4. Strike.

[33]*Vallejo Times-Herald*, September 6, 1969.
[34]Antioch police ask aid in wage talks. *Antioch Daily Ledger*, July 2, 1970, p. 1.
[35]*Ibid.*
[36]*Ibid.*

5. Refuse the increase and (based upon precedent) find it in their first paycheck of the fiscal year.

Dispite his reported unavailability, the city manager claimed that the municipality desired to continue negotiating and that, if he had violated anyone's constitutional rights, he would withdraw his statements. He told the press that he was attempting to contact the PORAC attorney.[37]

The city made its "final" offer of an 8½ percent pay raise on July 3rd; this was rejected by the police association. The objectionable conditions also were withdrawn by the city manager, but the police remained adamant, continuing to demand a 16 percent increase.[38] This relative impasse continued over the weekend. On July 6, the association decided to suspend legal action against the city manager (and the city) in order to keep negotiations alive. However, they accused the city of violating the state's Meyers-Milias-Brown Act.[39]

The police association unanimously voted on the night of July 6 to strike at 7:30 A.M., Saturday, July 11, if the city council continued to reject their offers for settlement. That same night, the city council met and voted to ask the public, by means of a referendum in November, for permission to levy additional taxes to pay for the salary increases (for all public employees) and add personnel (in all departments). The PORAC counsel was present at the meeting; he proposed that the police salary matter be put to mediation with the State Conciliation Board, to fact-finding, or to compulsory binding arbitration. He indicated that the only way to prevent the strike was to agree to mediation before it took place. He also indicated that the police officers would consider accepting a staggered increase. All of this, however, would have required $24,000 more than the budget included, and no agreement was forthcoming.[40]

The police chief's reaction to the strike vote was to announce he would inaugurate 12-hour shifts for the non-strikers: himself,

[37]City wants to talk. *Antioch Daily Ledger,* July 2, 1970, p. 1.
[38]City police reject "final" 8.5% hike. *Antioch Daily Ledger,* July 3, 1970, p. 1.
[39]Legal action is delayed. *Antioch Daily Ledger,* July 6, 1970, p. 1.
[40]Antioch police vote to strike Saturday; tax election planned. *Antioch Daily Ledger,* July 9, 1970, p. 1.

a captain, a lieutenant, and a dispatcher. They would be augmented by city management personnel. Once again, the city manager warned that a strike would have an adverse affect upon the voters in the upcoming November pay referendum.[41]

On Friday, July 10, the "haggling" between the police association and the city continued, and plans for protecting the city during the strike continued. The policemen indicated that they would not respond to any emergency once they went out on strike. Authorities stated that some legal complications existed relative to requesting county and/or state assistance. Also, the application of "mutual aid" provisions was not possible unless a civil disturbance occurred. No plans were made to declare a state of emergency unless an unforeseen major development were to occur. Meanwhile, the police association requested strike sanction from the Central Labor Council.[42]

The 23 policemen struck on Saturday morning, July 11. During the next two days, the Pittsburgh, California Police Association offered verbal support to the Antioch strikers and passed out leaflets.[43] Antioch's police station was manned by a city councilman and an administrative assistant, while other city management personnel assisted the three officers who remained on duty. No major police problems were encountered over the weekend. Pickets were posted at city hall, and PORAC donated $1,000 to the Antioch Police Strike Fund.[44]

On Monday, July 13, the third day of the strike, the 35-man Public Employees Union Local No. 1 staged a sick-in and failed to report for work at the city's corporation yards. While both sides expressed hope for an early settlement, no meetings had been held on Saturday or Sunday. Each side continued to blame the other for the strike.[45]

This second major police strike in California[46] (the first was in Vallejo in 1969) ended on July 14 after five hours of debate

[41]We'll work 12-hour shifts—Carlson. *Antioch Daily Ledger*, July 9, 1970, p. 1.
[42]City braces for police strike. *Antioch Daily Ledger*, July 10, 1970, p. 1.
[43]Pitt police back Antioch. *Antioch Daily Ledger*, July 13, 1970, p. 1.
[44]Police, city stalemated; yard workers are 'sick'. *Antioch Daily Ledger*, July 13, 1970, p. 1.
[45]*Ibid.*
[46]It wasn't easy, but strike's over. *Antioch Daily Ledger*, July 14, 1970, p. 1.

in a city council meeting. Police returned to duty at 2:30 A.M. after the council granted them a 12.25 percent pay increase, provided amnesty to police and other employees (corporation yard workers), and allowed all to charge their time off to accumulated overtime. Public Employees Union No. 1 was involved in the settlement in that they withdrew their demands for a one percent pay increase over that previously offered by the city. The settlement also included an agreement to not fill a vacant patrolman's position in order that the salary might be applied to the police wage increase.[47]

Police wages in Antioch, after the settlement, increased for a beginning patrolman to span from $771 per month to $933 per month; formerly the top rate was $829 each month. A senior patrolman's wage scale advanced to a range of $807 to $978 per month.[48]

THE HOLLISTER POLICE STRIKE

Following the example of Vallejo and Antioch, Hollister's 12-member police force went out on strike November 13, 1970, leaving public safety in the hands of its chief.[49] The previous day, the city council had rejected a demand by the policemen's association for a 10 percent pay increase. Although the council voted a 7½ percent boost, the seven patrolmen, three sergeants, and two matrons on the force walked off the job.[50] A call was put out to the San Benito County Sheriff's Office for help in any law enforcement problems.[51]

Hollister, a community of approximately 7,500 people, had a police monthly pay range of $584 to $710, which the association said was not in line with "going rates" in the area.[52]

A main street shooting occurred on November 16, but officials claimed the police strike had no relationship to the grudge assault. Sheriff's deputies handled the incident.[53]

[47]City police strike settled. *Antioch Daily Ledger*, July 14, 1970, p. 1.

[48]$1,200 more. *Antioch Daily Ledger*, July 14, 1970, p. 1.

[49]Chief patrols in Hollister police strike. *San Francisco Examiner*, November 13, 1970.

[50]Police force in Hollister calls strike. *Sacramento Bee*, November 13, 1970.

[51]*Ibid.*

[52]*Ibid.*

[53]Shooting in a copless town. *San Francisco Chronicle*, November 16, 1970.

The striking policemen returned to work on November 16 after a long session with the city manager, who warned that they would be subject to punitive action by the city council (this action could take the form of loss of pay or seniority). No concessions were made by the city. Actually, the strikers were fired on November 14, the second day of their walkout. They were allowed to return to work after the lengthy conference.[54]

Although the newspaper accounts do not show any activity on the part of PORAC in this strike, apparently that organization was involved. On November 24, the secretary of the Hollister Police Officers Association addressed a letter of thanks for PORAC's help during their recent strike.

[54]Hollister police back on the beat. *San Francisco Chronicle,* November 17, 1970.

Chapter V

DIGEST OF KNOWN POLICE UNION/ASSOCIATION ORGANIZATIONAL ACTIVITIES

The growth in local municipal employee associations in the United States from 1962 to 1968 shows an overall net increase of 50 percent. Total membership now exceeds one-quarter of a million employees.[1] The majority of these associations represent their members in matters of wages, working conditions, and the like. They also participate in legislative activities. Sixty-three percent of the local associations (representing 85% of the members) perform both functions.

Similarly, the *1969 Municipal Yearbook* shows that representation of police officers by organized labor-oriented bodies is increasing. The number of organized cities increased by 5 percent between 1966 and 1969. In terms of population groups, the greatest increase was in cities between 25,000 and 50,000 population; in terms of metropolitan status, the independent areas increased 11 percent. Organization in the Southern and North Central geographic regions increased 25 percent and 6 percent, respectively, while the Northeast and West decreased by 6 percent and 17 percent. Police union activity in cities with council-managers increased, whereas union activity in cities with mayor-council governments decreased. Cities with 100 percent membership remained the same during the period, but increases were noted in the percentage-membership groupings where membership was between 60 to 79 percent and over 90 percent.[2]

[1]Local association of municipal employees. *Urban Data Service,* International City Management Association, Vol. 2, No. 1, January 1970, passim.
[2]International City Management Association, *The Municipal Yearbook 1969.* Washington, D. C., International City Management Association, 1969, pp. 328-337.

The Fraternal Order of Police (FOP) still leads in the number of representative bodies; however, the American Federation of State, County and Municipal Employees is making significant gains. Representation by the AFSCME increased 97 percent between 1966 and 1969, with the greatest percentage increases in cities between 250,000 to 500,000 and 10,000 to 25,000 population, in suburban areas, in the Northeast, and in both mayor-council and council-manager forms of government. No-strike clauses in cities represented by the FOP increased 111 percent; in cities represented by the AFSCME these clauses increased 56 percent[3] (see Appendix A for 1970 abolishment of no-strike restriction).

Thus, evidence exists which proves that police employee organizations are fast becoming a significant voice in the relationships between policemen and city government. Police administrators can no longer ignore the activities of these organizations. The traditional feeling that police agencies are semi-military; and, police officers, by the very nature of their duties, are required to forego certain personal privileges enjoyed by employees in private industry no longer can be used as an excuse to disregard police unions. City officials must prepare to deal with them. Above all, police executives, who are caught in the middle of this controversy, must become prepared to initiate programs that will negate the need for such organizations or become equipped to cope with the consequences that may result from the intrusion of a union in the direct line of communication between the police executive and the beat patrolman.[4]

In the ensuing digest, information is presented on the national as well as on the state basis. Inquiries were addressed to labor and police officials in each state, and responses were received from only 22 percent—usable data from less than that. No response to inquiries were received by this researcher from Alabama, Alaska, Colorado, Connecticut, Delaware, Florida, Georgia, Indiana, Iowa, Kansas, Maryland, Massachusetts, Michigan, Missouri, Montana, Nebraska, Nevada, New Hampshire, New Jersey, New

3*Ibid.*
4*Ibid.*

Mexico, North Carolina, Ohio, Oklahoma, Oregon, Pennsylvania, Rhode Island, South Carolina, Texas, Utah, Vermont, West Virginia, Wisconsin, or Wyoming. Where no new answers or data were forthcoming, existing, available data is briefly presented. The best overall source for discussions of legal opinions and police official reactions to labor union affiliation of policemen remains the 1958 International Association of Chiefs of Police pamphlet.[5]

THE NATIONAL SCENE

The national scene includes the American Federation of State, County and Municipal Employees (AFL-CIO); International Brotherhood of Teamsters, Chauffeurs, Warehousemen, and Helpers of America; Fraternal Order of Police; and National Conference of Police Associations.

American Federation of State, County and Municipal Employees, AFL-CIO

Throughout the country, AFSCME represents approximately 11,000 police and sheriff's department employees. The federation maintains approximately 90 local unions (some 72% increase since 1958) in 20 states made up exclusively of such personnel. Membership in these locals approximates 10,000 police employees. An additional three dozen locals in 15 states represent police personnel along with other public employees.[6]

International Brotherhood of Teamsters, Chauffeurs, Warehousemen, and Helpers of America

The Teamsters represent 57,123 public employees, of which 4.1 percent, or 2,349 are engaged in providing police protection (see Appendix E).[7]

Fraternal Order of Police

The Fraternal Order of Police, founded in 1915, in 1945

[5]Carl E. Heustis, 1958, *op. cit.*, passim.
[6]Personal communication with Mr. D. S. Wasserman, Director, Department of Research, AFSCME, March 1971.
[7]Personal communication with Mr. A. Weiss, Director, Department of Research, Teamsters, November 1970.

claimed 163 Locals.[8] Twenty-four years later, it claims 900 locals and a membership of 90,000 policemen.[9]

National Conference of Police Associations

The National Conference of Police Associations appears to be a rival to the Fraternal Order of Police and, in 1958, claimed to include on its membership list local groups which represent 130,000 (approximately 32% of all policemen in the country) policemen in all sections of the country. It acts at the national level as a coordinating agency in matters of concern to all policemen.[10]

THE STATE SURVEY

Information contained in this survey was provided from responses to inquiries by this researcher from labor and public officials, in Arkansas, California, Hawaii, Idaho, Illinois, Kentucky, Louisiana, Maine, Minnesota, Mississippi, North Dakota, South Dakota, Tennessee, Virginia, and Washington. Other information relating to the states who failed to respond was obtained from available written sources.

Alabama

A ruling of the Alabama attorney general on September 19, 1946, upheld the authority of a municipality to prohibit membership of policemen in a labor union and held that a municipality had no authority to enter into contract with or recognize a union.[11]

In 1953, the Alabama Legislature adopted a law providing penalties for any employee of the state who joins or participates in a labor union or a labor organization.[12]

Arkansas

Prior to 1957, policemen in Little Rock were union organized; but, in the 1957 session of the Arkansas Legislature, House Bill

---

[8]Emma Schweppe: *The Firemen's and Patrolmen's Unions in the City of New York.* New York, King's Crown Press, 1948, p. 1.

[9]M. W. Aussieker, Jr., *op. cit.*, p. 12.

[10]Carl E. Heustic, 1958, *op. cit.*, p. 6.

[11]*Ibid.*, p. 11.

[12]*Ibid.*, pp. 23-24.

3 became law. This bill prohibited policemen from holding membership in a labor organization. Subsequently, the constitutionality of the measure was challenged in *Potts v. Hayes;* and, the Arkansas Supreme Court declared the measure unconstitutional. However, no effort has been made to revive the police union movement.[13]

California

See Chapter IV, "The California Scene."

Colorado

In 1958, Denver and Pueblo each had police unions affiliated with the AFL, which had official recognition.[14]

Connecticut

At least nine police unions exist in Connecticut: Bridgeport, East Haven, Harden, Hartford, Meriden, Milford, Naugatuck, New Britain, and New Haven. All are affiliated with the AFL and are officially recognized.[15]

Georgia

Law enforcement labor unions are prohibited by a law adopted by the Georgia Legislature in November 1953.[16]

Hawaii

A Collective Bargaining Law for Public Employees has been enacted by the legislature; it became effective on January 1, 1971. The Governor has appointed three men to serve on the five-member Hawaii Public Employment Relations Board, which will operate similarly to the NLRB.[17]

The two major government employees unions in Hawaii are the Hawaii Government Employees Association and the United Public Workers, both affiliated with the AFSCME. The former

[13]Personal communication with Mr. J. B. Becker, President, Arkansas State AFL-CIO, November 1970.

[14]Carl E. Heustis, 1958, *op. cit.*, p. 18.

[15]*Ibid.*, p. 20.

[16]*Ibid.*, p. 24.

[17]Personal communication with Mr. B. D. Kaye, Director of Research, Hawaii State Federation of Labor, AFL-CIO, November 1970 and January 1971.

claims approximately 19,000 members and the latter approximately 8,500.[18]

Law enforcement is a county responsibility, and authorities expect that policemen will affiliate with a labor union.[19]

Idaho

Idaho has reported one police union in the state—Teamsters Local 551 in Lewiston. This local also has collective bargaining agreements with the cities of Pullman and Clarkston in the state of Washington. Its contracts include no-strike clauses.[20]

Illinois

Inquiries of this researcher were referred to the National Headquarters of AFSCME. However, Illinois authorities indicated three or four police locals with a local charter that may still be active.[21] In 1958, nine police unions were reported (Alton, Aurora, Belleville, Bloomington, East St. Louis, Elgin, Joliet, Rock Island, and Springfield).[22]

Kentucky

Apparently no organized labor attempt has been made to unionize police in Kentucky. However, lodges affiliated with the Fraternal Order of Police do exist in Louisville.[23]

Louisiana

Two police unions exist; one in Bogalusa, and one in Monroe. The former is affiliated with the Office Employees Union and the latter with AFSCME. Almost all of the other cities in Louisiana have recently organized local unions affiliated with the

18*Ibid.*

19*Ibid.*

20Personal communication with Mr. R. W. Macfarlane, President, Idaho State AFL-CIO, November 1970.

21Personal communication with Mr. S. L. Johnson, President, Illinois State Federation of Labor and Congress of Industrial Organizations, November 1970.

22Carl E. Heustis, 1958, *op. cit.,* p. 20.

23Personal communication with Mr. H. C. Lake, Director, Department of Research and Education, Kentucky State AFL-CIO, November 1970.

embryonic International Brotherhood of Police Officers, which is seeking an AFL-CIO charter.[24]

Maine

Eight police organizations affiliated with the AFSCME were reported. These are in Augusta, Bangor, Fairfield, Gardiner, Rumford, South Portland, Waterville, and Westbrook. One non-affiliated organization exists in Portland—the Police Benefit Association.[25]

Maine has recently enacted a Municipal Public Employees Labor Relations Law. It became effective on February 9, 1970, and has resulted in active organizing by the AFSCME.[26]

District of Columbia

The District of Columbia code spells out prohibitions regarding affiliation with certain organizations by members of the Metropolitan Police Department, which for all practical purposes bars police unions.[27]

Massachusetts

Two hundred fifty-nine Springfield policemen staged a "blue flu" sick-out on January 14, 1971 to protest the lack of progress in negotiations with the city for a new contract. They returned to work the following night in response to a court order.[28]

Departmental rules and regulations prohibit state police unions.[29]

Michigan

In 1967, 870 members of the 4,400-man Detroit Police Department entered into a "sick call" strike. Two hundred forty-four were suspended, and the tactic ended the next day. Two months

---

[24]Personal communication with Mr. V. Bussie, President, Louisiana AFL-CIO, November 1970.

[25]Personal communication with Mr. C. J. O'Leary, Special Assistant to the President, Maine State Federated Labor Council, AFL-CIO, November 1970.

[26]*Ibid.*

[27]Carl E. Heustis, 1958, *op. cit.,* p. 25.

[28]Absent police return to duty in Springfield. *Sacramento Bee,* January 16, 1971.

[29]Carl E. Heustis, 1958, *op. cit.,* p. 18.

later, the city signed a collective bargaining agreement with the Detroit Police Officers' Association. The mayor hailed the agreement as "a milestone in labor relations since it marks the first agreement of its kind ever made between a municipal government and its local police officers."[30]

In 1958, Michigan reported four police unions with AFL-CIO affiliations: Flint, Lansing, Muskegon, and Muskegon Heights. All but Muskegon had official recognition.[31]

Minnesota

Minnesota has several police locals in the state affiliated with the AFSCME.[32] In 1958, there were three AFL-affiliated police unions: Duluth, Hopkins, and St. Paul. All had official recognition.[33]

Mississippi

One local of the International Brotherhood of Police Officers in Biloxi is seeking to affiliate with Mississippi AFL-CIO, pending receipt of a national AFL-CIO charter.[34]

The Mississippi Supreme Court has upheld the authority of municipal governments to prohibit membership in a police union.[35]

Missouri

The Missouri Supreme Court has upheld the authority of municipal governments to prohibit membership in a police union.[36]

Nebraska

In 1958, Omaha had a police union affiliated with the AFL, included all ranks; however, it had no official recognition.[37]

[30]A labor milestone for police. *The Sacramento Union*, August 23, 1967.

[31]Carl E. Heustis, 1958, *op. cit.*, p. 20.

[32]Personal communication with Mr. M. McNeff, Public Information Director, Minnesota AFL-CIO Federation of Labor, Noverber 1970.

[33]Carl E. Heustis, 1958, *op. cit.*, p. 20.

[34]Personal communication with Mr. C. Ramsey, President, Mississippi AFL-CIO, December 1970.

[35]Carl E. Heustis, 1958, *op. cit.*, pp. 39-41.

[36]*Ibid.*

[37]*Ibid.*, p. 20.

New Jersey

New Jersey has a statewide Police Benevolent Association with local chapters in the various town, municipal, and county police agencies.[38] However, departmental rules and regulations prohibit a state police union.[39]

New York

New York is one of the most active areas in the nation as regards police unionization. What occurs there is of significance to the entire nation since it is one of the pace-setting locales of the country.

In 1967, the state of New York passed the Public Employees Fair Employment Act. For the first time in any state, all governmental entities were granted the right to organize, be represented, negotiate the terms and conditions of their employment, and enter into contracts with their employers. The employer is required to recognize the employee representative, negotiate, contract and live up to the contract, and to refrain from interfering with all employment rights of employees.[40] As a consequence, the New York State Police now have union representation through the New York State Police Benevolent Association which acts as the collective bargaining agent; the Association recently negotiated a two-year contract with a no-strike clause.[41]

The city of New York experienced its first police strike in January 1971. For six days and five nights, some 25,000 patrolmen defied the law by refusing to work. The striking patrolmen walked out over a back-pay issue, overriding pleas of leaders from their bargaining organization—the Patrolmen's Benevolent Association. A vote of PBA precinct delegates sent the strikers back to their beats, as a court trial on the pay claim got under way.[42]

[38]*Ibid.*, p. 6.

[39]*Ibid.*, p. 18.

[40]*The Police Yearbook of 1970*. Washington, D. C., International Association of Chiefs of Police, 1970, p. 100.

[41]For a complete treatment of the subject, see William E. Kirwan: *The New York State Police: History and Development of Collective Negotiations*. Albany, New York, Superintendent, New York State Police, 1969.

[42]When police walked out in New York. *U. S. News and World Report*, February 1, 1971, p. 42.

The city, with its skeletonized protection, escaped the ominous upsurge of crime that terrorized Montreal in 1969 and Boston in 1919 when police in those cities went out on strike. Of the strike, the *New York Times* editorialized:[43]

> The disgraceful desertion of duty by the vast majority of the city's patrolmen has ended . . . But the relief New Yorkers must feel at the belated return to regard for law by the sworn upholders of the law is shadowed by an awareness that the existing truce is a tenuous one, subject to upset whenever bluecoated militants decide once again they can cow the city by violating their oaths and exposing their fellow citizens to potential disaster.

North Carolina

In 1958, the cities of Asheville and Durham had AFL-affiliated police unions which were not officially recognized.[44]

North Dakota

The policemen in the city of Fargo, 53,000 population, are organized in Local 116 of the Teamsters Union.[45]

Ohio

In 1958, Massilon had an AFL-affiliated police union which was not officially recognized.[46]

Ohio state law, while not specifically prohibiting police union organization, placed rigid interpretations on police duties which render refusal to perform statutory duties a criminal offense, thus denying the right to strike. A number of Ohio cities recognize local chapters of the Fraternal Order of Police as spokesmen for the local police.[47]

Oregon

In 1958, Portland had an AFL-affiliated police union which was officially recognized.[48]

[43]*Ibid.*
[44]Carl E. Heustis, 1958, *op. cit.,* p. 20.
[45]Personal communication with Mr. W. J. Dockter, President, North Dakota AFL-CIO, December 1970.
[46]Carl E. Heustis, 1958, *op. cit.,* p. 20.
[47]*Ibid.,* p. 25.
[48]*Ibid.,* p. 20.

Pennsylvania

Pennsylvania State Police are represented by the Fraternal Order of Police, who played a part in moving Pennsylvania from fourth to first among states with the highest state police salary scales on July 1, 1971.[49]

South Dakota

No police unionization effort appears under way at this time at any level in South Dakota, although Fraternal Order of Police Lodges exist at the city level along with the South Dakota Peace Officers' Association at the state level.[50] However, in 1958, an officially recognized AFL-affiliated police union existed in Huron.[51]

Tennessee

Apparently only two police unions exist in Tennessee: the Policeman's Assistance League in Nashville and AFSCME Local No. 644 in Hixson.[52] However, in 1958, Chattanooga had an officially recognized AFL-affiliated police union.[53]

Texas

A civil service statute prohibits the use of the strike by police and fire department employees.[54]

Virginia

The only incidence of police organization is in Portsmouth; apparently affiliated with AFSCME.[55]

Virginia prohibits the use of the strike to any police employee in the state.[56]

[49]Pennsylvania State Police's pay raise. *San Francisco Chronicle,* December 25, 1970.

[50]Personal communication with Mr. C. W. Shrader, President, South Dakota AFL-CIO, November 1970.

[51]Carl E. Heustis, 1958, *op. cit.,* p. 20.

[52]Personal communication with the Tennessee State Labor Council, November 1970.

[53]Carl E. Heustis, 1958, *op. cit.,* p. 20.

[54]*Ibid.,* p. 24.

[55]Personal communication with Mr. B. Snow, Secretary-Treasurer, Virginia State AFL-CIO, November 1970.

[56]Carl E. Heustis, 1958, *op. cit.,* p. 26.

Washington

At one time, almost all police personnel in the state of Washington were affiliated with the AFSCME; however, internal conflicts erupted and most of the police unions disaffiliated, with only two locals remaining in the AFL-CIO (one is Tacoma Local No. 224). Some deputy sheriffs also are affiliated with the AFSCME, the Teamsters, and the Building Service Employees Union.[57] Apparently, affiliation with the FOP has occurred at least in Spokane.[58] Two cities, Pullman and Clarkston, have collective bargaining arrangements with Teamsters Local No. 551 located in Lewiston, Idaho.[59]

Wisconsin

The Milwaukee Professional Policemen's Protective Association represents all but 42 of the 2,100-member police force. On January 23, 1971, 95 percent of Milwaukee's policemen remained at home with the "blue flu" over a dispute regarding wages and grievance procedures.[60]

The Wisconsin State Patrol is organized as a local, affiliated with AFSCME.[61]

In 1958, the city of La Crosse had an officially recognized AFL-affiliated police union.[62]

[57]Personal communication with Mr. S. Kinville, Government Affairs Director, Washington State Labor Council, AFL-CIO, November 1970.
[58]Carl E. Heustis, 1958, *op. cit.*, p. 10.
[59]*Infra*, p.
[60]Most of Milwaukee police ill. *San Francisco Chronicle*, January 24, 1971.
[61]Carl E. Heustis, 1958, *op. cit.*, pp. 7-8.
[62]*Ibid.*, p. 20.

Chapter VI

DIGEST OF STATE LEGAL AUTHORITY
RELATING TO EMPLOYEE/UNION ACTIVITIES

In terms of both statutory and case law, several very significant current questions seem pertinent: Do public employees, including policemen, have the right to organize and join employee organizations and labor unions? Do these employees possess the right to collectively bargain? Do they have the right to strike? To what extent are appropriate labor management tools used in the settlement of labor grievances and labor-management disputes? What trends are indicated through current proposed legislation in the states? To the degree that data is available, this chapter is an attempt to answer these important questions.

RIGHT TO ORGANIZE AND JOIN

Table I presents a summary of state legal authority for public employees to organize and join employee organizations and labor unions. Only two states, Alabama and Missouri, offer any kind of prohibitions. The Code of Alabama, Title 37, Art. 7, Sec. 450 (1), (2) gives state and municipal fire fighters the right to join any labor organization so long as the organization does not advocate the right to strike. In Missouri, Vernon's Annotated Missouri Statutes, Sec. 105.500, permits the organization and the joining of labor unions to all public employees, with the exception of law enforcement personnel and teachers. Twenty (40%) of the states specifically grant all public employees the right to organize and join employee organizations of their own choosing. Twenty-nine (57%) are silent on the subject.

In addition to state statutes, restrictions against policemen organizing and joining employee organizations are found in municipal ordinances and departmental regulations. Prior to 1968, the trend of the decisions in the state courts was to uphold

TABLE I*

STATE LEGAL AUTHORITY TO ORGANIZE AND JOIN EMPLOYEE ORGANIZATIONS AND LABOR UNIONS

State	Right to Organize			State Legal Authority
	Silent	Yes	No	
Alabama			X	
Alaska	X			
Arizona	X			
Arkansas	X			
California		X		Calif. Government Code, Sec. 3500
Colorado	X			
Connecticut	X			
Delaware	X			Delaware Code Annot. Title 19, Ch. 13, Sec. 1301 *et al.*
Dist. of Columbia	X			
Florida		X		Florida Constitution Art. 1, Sec. 6
Georgia	X			
Hawaii	X			
Idaho	X			
Illinois		X		*Chicago Div. of Educ. Assoc. vs. Board of Ed.* 222 NE 2d 243
Indiana		X		Attorney General's Opinion (1944)
Iowa	X			
Kansas	X			
Kentucky	X			
Louisiana		X		Attorney General's Opinion, October 1969 (policemen only)
Maine		X		Maine Rev. Statutes, Title 26, Ch. 9a, Sec. 961 *et al.*
Maryland	X			
Massachusetts		X		Massachusetts Law Annot., Ch. 763, Sec. 178 F, Sec. G-N.
Michigan		X		Michigan Statutes Annot. 17.455 (1) *et al.*
Minnesota		X		Minnesota Statutes Annot. Sec. 179.50 *et al.*
Mississippi	X			
Missouri			X	Vernon's Annot. Statutes Sec. 105.500 prohibits firemen and policemen.
Montana	X			
Nebraska		X		Reissue Rev. Statutes of Nebraska 48-801 *et al.*
Nevada		X		Nevada Statutes
New Hampshire		X		N.H. Rev. Statutes Annot., Ch. 31, Sec. 3, granted to towns.
New Mexico		X		*Int. Brotherhood of Electrical Workers vs. Farmington* 405 P 2d 233
New Jersey		X		New Jersey Constitution Art. 1, Sec. 19
New York		X		McKinney's Consolidated Laws of N.Y., Civil Service Law Sec. 200
North Carolina	X			
North Dakota		X		(Teachers Only) N.D. Century Code Annot. Ch. 15-38.1
Ohio	X			
Oklahoma	X			
Oregon		X		Oregon Rev. Statutes 662.715
Pennsylvania	X			
Rhode Island		X		General Laws of Rhode Island, 36-11-1 *et al.*
South Carolina	X			

*Adapted from John H. Burpo, *The Police Union Movement.* Springfield, Charles C Thomas, pp. 39-60.

South Dakota	X	South Dakota Compiled Law Annot., Sec. 3-18-1 *et al.*
Tennessee	X	
Texas	X	
Utah	X	
Vermont	X	
Virginia	X	
Washington	X	
West Virginia	X	
Wisconsin	X	
Wyoming		X	Wyoming Statutes, Cr. 11, Sec. 27-265 *et al.*

these restrictions on the ground that the policeman is in an unusual position in society and may be denied rights under the First Amendment that are available to other citizens.[1]

On the other hand, not all cases prior to 1968 were rulings against the policeman's right to organize and join employee organizations; a few state courts held that the policeman did have the right to organize and join an organization of his choosing.[2] These cases were based, however, on existing state constitutional and statutory provisions clearly granting public employees this right.[3]

Current law stems from two Federal Circuit Court cases decided in 1968 and 1969. In citing these cases Burpo has said:[4]

Federal Circuit court cases in 1968 and 1969 may be cited on the general proposition that the First Amendment confers a right on all public employees to form and join a union or other type of employee organization, including policemen. This interpretation has received support from most commentators on public labor problems.[6] Although these cases represent the opinions of the Seventh and Eighth Federal Circuits, it is a

[1]*City of Jackson v. McLeod* 24 So 2d 319 (1946).

[2]*Beverly v. City of Dallas* 292 SW 2d 172; *Le Vasseur v. Wheelden* 112 NW 849 (1962); *Potts v. Hay* 318 SW 2d 826 (1958).

[3]For example in the Arkansas case of *Petts v. Hay,* the State Supreme Court held that the State Constitution's requirement that no person shall be denied employment because of the membership in a labor union applies to all public employees.

[4]John H. Burpo: *The Police Labor Movement.* Springfield, Charles C Thomas Publisher, 1971, p. 62.

[5]Report of the IACP Special Committee on Police Employee Organizations: Police employee organizations. *The Police Chief,* December 1969, p. 54.

TABLE II*

STATE LEGAL AUTHORITY FOR PUBLIC EMPLOYEE COLLECTIVE BARGAINING

State	Right to Bargain		Legal Authority
	Yes	No	
Alabama		X	*Int. Union of Operating Engineers Local vs. Waterworks Board of Birmingham*, 55 L.R.N.N. 2950 (1964).
Alaska	X		Alaska Statutes, Ch. 40, Sec. 23-40.010.
Arizona	X		*Local 226 vs. Salt Water Project Agr. Imp. Dist.*
Arkansas		X	*City of Ft. Smith vs. Ark. State Counsel* 38 433 SW 2d 153.
California	X		California Government Code, Sec. 3500 *et al.*
Colorado		X	*Fellows vs. Catronica* 327 P 2d 547 (1962).
Connecticut	X		Connecticut General Statutes Annot. Sec. 7-467.
Delaware	X		Delaware Code Annot., Title 19, Ch. 13, Sec. 1301.
Wash. D. C.	X		Federal Executive Order 11491.
Florida		X	*Dade County vs. Amalgomated Assoc. of St. Elec. Railway and Motor Coach Employees of Amer.* 157 So. 2d 176.
Georgia		X	*Int. Longshoremen's Assoc. vs. Georgia P.A.* 124 SE 2d 783.
Hawaii	X		Senate Bill 1696-70 (1970).
Idaho		X	*Local 283 Int. Bro. of Elect. Workers vs. Robinson* 423 P 2d 999.
Illinois	X		*Chicago Div. of Ed. Assoc. vs. Board of Ed.* 222 NE 2d 243.
Kansas		X	*Wichita Public Schools Employees Union Local No. 513 vs. Wichita* 397 P 2d 357 (1964).
Kentucky		X	*Firemen & Oilers vs. Board of Ed.* 59 L.R.R.M. 2564 (1965).
Louisiana	X		Louisiana Revised Statutes 23-890.
Maine	X		Maine Revised Statutes, Title 26, Ch. 9A, Sec. 961.
Massachusetts	X		Massachusetts Law Annot., Ch. 793, Secs. 178F-Secs.G-N.
Michigan	X		Michigan Statutes Annot., 17450 (1) *et al.*
Minnesota	X		Minnesota Statutes Annot., Sec. 179.50 *et al.*
Missouri		X	Vernon's Missouri Statutes Annot., 105.500 *et al.*
Nebraska	X		Reissue Rev. Statutes of Nebraska 48-801 *et al.*
Nevada	X		Nevada Statutes.
New Hampshire	X		New Hampshire Rev. Statutes Annot., Ch. 31, Sec. 3.
New Mexico	X		*Int. Bro. of Elect. Workers vs. Farmington*, 405 P 2d 233 (1965).
New Jersey	X		New Jersey Statutes Annot., Ch. 303 13A *et al.*
New York	X		McKinney's Con. Laws of N.Y., Civil Service Law Sec. 200 *et al.*
North Carolina		X	Gen. Statutes of North Carolina, Sec. 95-97 *et al.*
North Dakota		X	North Dakota Century Code Annot., Ch. 15-38-1.
Ohio		X	*Building Service and Maintenance Union Local 47 vs. St. Lukes Hospital* 277 NE 2d 256 (1967).
Oregon	X		Oregon Rev. Statutes, Sec. 243, 710 *et al.*
Pennsylvania	X		Purdons Stat. Annot., Ch. 43, Sec. 217.1, Tit. 55, Sec 563.2.
Rhode Island	X		General Law of Rhode Island, 36-11-5.
South Dakota	X		South Dakota Compiled Law Annot., 3-18-1 *et al.*
Tennessee		X	*Weakley County Munic. Elec. System vs. Vick*, 309 SW 2d 782.
Texas		X	Vernon's Texas Civil Statutes Annot., Art. 51540.
Vermont	X		23 Vermont Statutes Annot., 901 *et al.*
Washington	X		Rev. Code of Washington Annot., 44, 56, 010 *et al.*
Wisconsin	X		Wisconsin Stat. Annot., Sec. 111.80 *et al;* III.70 *et al.*
Wyoming	X		Wyoming Statutes, Ch. 11, Sec. 27-265 *et al.*

*Adapted from John H. Burpo, *The Police Union Movement.* Springfield, Charles C Thomas, pp. 39-60.

virtual certainty that they will be followed as authority by most courts in the land today.[6]

RIGHT TO COLLECTIVE BARGAINING

Table II indicates that state legal authority for public employee collective bargaining is provided through both statutory and case law. It further indicates that the right is currently denied in some states through this same law. Twenty-seven of the states and the District of Columbia (54%) have provided the right to collectively bargain; 15 (29%) clearly deny public employees this right; nine (17%) have no statutes or case law on the subject.

In all of the states (27) where the right is recognized, specific statutes have been provided which grant this right. In other states that deny the right (15), the denial has come through state court decisions. No U. S. Supreme Court nor Federal Appellate case decisions have been rendered which limit or set aside state statutory or case law relating to collective bargaining. Thus, the stand taken by 41 states and the District of Columbia, whether the particular state grants or denies collective bargaining to public employees, appears to be a legal one.

Some speculation exists as to the right of public employees to collective bargaining in the nine states that provide no statutory or case law on the subject. Since 15 states have outlawed collective bargaining and 27 have legalized it, it appears that—in the nine states in question—the need is for statutory or case law, either granting or denying the right.

RIGHT TO STRIKE

Table III indicates the status of state statutory and case law on the legal authority of public employees to strike. Of the 50 states and the District of Columbia, the law clearly denies all public employees the right to strike in 18 jurisdictions (35.5%). In 32 of the states (63%) the law is silent on the matter.

Only one state, Hawaii, has provided legislation legalizing public employee strikes. During the 1970 legislative session, the

[6]For example, the North Carolina Federal District Court held in 1969 that firemen cannot be prohibited from joining a labor union, *Atkins v. City of Charlotte* 290 F. Supp. 1068 (1969).

TABLE III*
STATE LEGAL AUTHORITY FOR PUBLIC EMPLOYEE STRIKES

State	Silent	Yes	No	State Legal Authority
				(Right to Strike)
Alabama			X	Code of Alabama, Title 37, Art. 7, Sec. 450 (1), (2).
Alaska	X			
Arizona	X			
Arkansas	X			
California			X	
Colorado	X			
Connecticut	X			
Delaware			X	Delaware Code Annot., Title 19, Ch. 13, Sec. 1301 et al.
Wash. D. C.			X	(Police) D. C. Code Annot., Sec. 4-125.
Florida			X	Florida Statutes Annot. Sec. 838.221.
Georgia			X	Code of Georgia Annot. Sec. 89-1301 et al.
Hawaii		X		Senate Bill 1696170.
Idaho	X			
Illinois	X			
Indiana	X			
Iowa	X			
Kansas	X			
Kentucky	X			
Louisiana			X	Attorney General's Opinion, October 1969.
Maine	X			
Maryland	X			
Massachusetts		X		Mass. Law Annot., Ch. 763, Secs. G-N.
Michigan		X		Mich. Statutes Annot., 17.455 (1) et al.
Minnesota		X		Minn. Statutes Annot., Sec. 179.50 et al.
Mississippi	X			
Missouri			X	Mo. Statutes Sec. 105.500 et al.
Montana	X			
Nebraska	X			
Nevada			X	Nevada Statutes.
New Hampshire	X			
New Mexico	X			
New Jersey			X	Art. 1. Sec. 19 N.J. Constitution; N.J. Statutes Annot. Ch. 303 13 A et al.
New York			X	McKinney's Cons. Laws of N.Y., Civil Service Law Sec. 200.
North Carolina	X			
North Dakota	X			
Ohio			X	Ohio Rev. Code, Labor and Industry, Ch. 4117, Sec. .01 et al.
Oklahoma	X			
Oregon	X			
Pennsylvania	X			
Rhode Island	X			
South Carolina	X			
South Dakota	X			
Tennessee			X	*City of Alcoa vs. Int. Brotherhood of Electrical Workers* 308 SW 2d 749 (1958).
Texas			X	Vernon's Civil Statutes Tex. Annot., Art. 515C.
Utah	X			
Vermont	X			
Virginia			X	Code of Virginia, Sec. 40-65 et al.
Washington	X			
West Virginia	X			
Wisconsin	X			
Wyoming	X			

*Adapted from John H. Burpo, *The Police Union Movement.* Springfield, Charles C Thomas, pp. 39-60.

state adopted a collective bargaining law giving all public employees the right to negotiate and to strike when all impasse procedures fail.[7]

State public employee anti-strike laws in 18 states continue to retain their validity.

In October of 1971 the U.S. Supreme Court, in *United Federation of Postal Clerks v. United States,* affirmed the judgment of the U.S. District Court of the District of Columbia. It stated, in essence, that federal workers have the right to organize and bargain collectively but do not have the "constitutional" right to strike. Further, the court said that it is not "irrational" or "arbitrary" for the Federal Government to prohibit strikes on the part of its workers. Although this case involved federal employees, authorities also agree that it is the controlling case in questions of the right of other public employees to strike. Clearly the case upholds the right of other governmental entities to deny public employees the right to strike.

In turn, the rationale behind these laws remains the same as that advanced by public officials and police administrators in 1919, 1944, and 1958. Additionally, the majority of police strikes and other forms of work stoppages have been conducted by employee groups not affiliated with organized labor.[8] As Burpo puts it, "the strike and other forms of work stoppage are employed equally, if not more, by fraternal and benevolent associations."[9] He further states:

> When policemen conduct work stoppage, the usual reason is all other methods of achieving a better wage or improved job conditions have failed. Negotiations have proven unsuccessful, and the forms of protest short of work stoppage have been unavailing. When all avenues of redress have been exhausted, the police see no alternative but to strike. The lack of alternatives does not justify this conduct, but does point to the critical need for feasible alternatives to be devised in lieu of the strike.[10]

[7]Senate Bill 1969-1970.

[8]Hervy Juris: *The Implications of Police Unions for Policing.* University of Wisconsin Press, 1969, p. 9.

[9]Burpo, *op. cit.,* p. 80.

[10]*Ibid.,* pp. 80-81.

LEGAL EXTENT OF USE OF LABOR MANAGEMENT TOOLS

Table II established the fact that 27 of the 50 states and the District of Columbia (54%) provide some sort of law which legalizes public employee collective bargaining, either through statutes or court decisions. Table IV indicates the extent to which the law in these 27 collective bargaining states furnish the additional tools necessary to the settlement of public employee labor disputes: mediation, fact-finding, advisory arbitration, and mandatory (compulsory) arbitration.

Obviously, the 23 noncollective bargaining states provide for none of these devices. Of the 27 collective bargaining states, two provide for mediation only; three, fact-finding only; one provides advisory arbitration for fire fighters only; three provide

TABLE IV*

EXTENT OF MEDIATION, FACT-FINDING, AND ARBITRATION
IN COLLECTIVE BARGAINING STATES

State	None	Mediation	Fact-finding	Advisory Arbitration	Compulsory Arbitration
Alabama	X				
Alaska	X				
California		X			
Connecticut		X	X	X	
Delaware		X		X	
D. C.		X		X	
Hawaii	X				
Illinois	X				
Louisiana					X
Maine		X	X		
Mass.			X	X	
Michigan		X			
Minn.		X		X	
Nebraska			X		
Nevada		X	X		
N. H.	X				
N. M.	X				
N. J.		X	X		
New York		X	X		
Oregon			X		
Penna. (for police only)					X
R. I.					X
S. D.	X				
Vermont		X	X		
Wash.	X				
Wisconsin		X	X		
Wyoming (for fire-fighters)				X	

*Adapted from John H. Burpo, *The Police Union Movement.* Springfield, Charles C Thomas, pp. 39-60.

compulsory arbitration (one of these for policemen only); seven states offer both mediation and fact-finding; two others offer fact-finding and advisory arbitration (one of these, for fire fighters only); only one state (Connecticut) offers mediation, fact-finding and advisory arbitration; only three states (Louisiana, Rhode Island and Pennsylvania) provide for compulsory arbitration (one of these, Pennsylvania, offers compulsory arbitration for police only). Of the entire group of collective bargaining states, eight offer none of the settlement tools common to industrial, labor-management relations.

THE TREND IN LABOR LEGISLATION

The trend in labor legislation is dramatically illustrated in Table V. It presents a summary of legislative proposals relating to public employee labor problems as presented to state legislatures in a single year—1969. At least one piece of proposed legislation was submitted to the legislative bodies of 17 of the 50 states; in a number of these jurisdictions several bills were introduced.

TABLE V*

PROPOSED STATE LEGISLATION RELATING TO PUBLIC
EMPLOYEE LABOR PROBLEMS (1969)

State	Subject Matter	Passed	Failed
Alabama	Power to organize; collectively bargain		X
Alaska	Mandatory collective bargaining		X
Colorado	Power to collectively bargain; strike		X
Indiana	Right to enter agreements; collectively bargain		X
Iowa	Right to enter agreements; to bargain		X
Kansas	Right to collectively bargain		X
Maine	Repealed firefighter's arbitration law	X	
Maryland	Prohibited work stoppages and strikes		X
Michigan	Mandatory arbitration—police and firemen	X	
Montana	Provided collective bargaining; prohibited bargaining with labor unions		X
Nevada	Collective bargaining; mediation, fact-finding		X
New Mexico	Collective bargaining; mediation or voluntary arbitration		X
Ohio	Collective bargaining for police and firemen; compulsory arbitration—all public employees		X
Pennsylvania	Collective bargaining; injunction procedures on work stoppages		X
South Dakota	Collective bargaining; voluntary arbitration		X
Texas	Firemen's right to mediate disputes		X
Washington	Collective bargaining	X	

*Adapted from John H. Burpo, *The Police Union Movement.* Springfield, Charles C Thomas, pp. 39-60.

The bills ran the gamut of public employee labor problems: the right to organize and join labor organizations, the right to collectively bargain, mandatory collective bargaining, mediation, fact-finding, advisory arbitration, compulsory arbitration, injunction procedures on work stoppages, and work stoppages and strikes.

Public employee labor legislation was adopted in only three of the states; in Maine, legislation repealed an existing fire fighter's arbitration law; Michigan provided mandatory arbitration for police and firemen, and Washington passed collective bargaining legislation for all public employees. All public employee labor bills introduced in Alabama, Alaska, Colorado, Indiana, Iowa, Kansas, Maryland, Montana, Nevada, New Mexico, Ohio, Pennsylvania, South Dakota, and Texas went down in defeat.

Some interesting but distressing conclusions can be drawn; (1) the majority of state legislation currently proposed is destined for defeat, and (2) a major portion of this legislation is destined for defeat, regardless of the subject matter or problems involved. These conclusions are fortified through the experience of Pennsylvania where a bill providing for injunction procedures on work stoppages was defeated—again in Maryland where the proposed law prohibited work stoppages and strikes.

Chapter VII

HISTORICAL AND CONTEMPORARY CONSIDERATIONS AFFECTING POLICE UNIONS

While it appears to be generally conceded that cause exists for the average policeman to be dissatisfied with his employment conditions and the effectiveness of his local police association, police and public officials cling to a myth: the ideal of service prevents the policeman and the police administrator from supporting the police union concept. As the International Association of Chiefs of Police summed it up in its 1958 bulletin:[1]

> . . . the labor union concept as applied to the police service seems incompatible. Where the question has been passed upon by jurists, corporation counsels, city commissions or councils, or other responsible public bodies, the prevalent majority opinion appears to be that police unions, affiliated with trade-labor organizations, are:
> 1. Contrary to the basic nature of police duties;
> 2. Powerless to engage in collective bargaining or benefit from the closed shop, check-off system, or strike privileges; and
> 3. Subject to the constitutional authority of state and municipal governments to adopt a policy prohibiting police employees from such affiliation.
> The majority of police administrators concur in this opinion. Through all of the rulings and decisions issued on the subject of police unions, there appears the general conclusion that police officers, by the very nature of their duties, are required to forego certain personal privileges enjoyed by employees in private industry. It is a premise that any delegation of authority vested in public officers, not sanctioned by law, is an act violating our constitutional mandates. It follows that no police chief or other official may legally surrender or relinquish his unfettered control of the police department to meet the demands of a union. A democratic system of government depends upon the unbiased

[1]Carl E. Heustis, 1958, *op. cit.*, p. 3.

and impartial enforcement of law adopted by the people through constitutional processes and the unquestioned loyalty and devotion to duty of the men who are entrusted with this most important branch of the democratic government.

Without a doubt, this is the same unrealistic position that has been taken by American leaders since the Boston police strike of 1919—even those prominent politicians otherwise noted for their liberal and pro-labor positions. In 1937, Franklin D. Roosevelt said of strikes against the government:[2]

A strike of public employees manifests nothing less than an attempt to prevent or obstruct the operations of government until their demands are satisfied. Such action, looking toward the paralysis of government by those who have sworn to support it, is unthinkable and intolerable.

Yet, despite this widespread sentiment, public policy regarding the unionization of government employees is in the process of change. Existing evidence proves that municipal and state government workers are seeking to affiliate with the organized labor movement in ever-increasing numbers. Moreover, equal evidence proves that the laws prohibiting this collective bargaining are being relaxed or abandoned in many of the leading states.

Thus, some far-reaching considerations now warrant special attention. The most paramount of these are the following:[3]

1. The legal competence of state and municipal units to enter into collective bargaining agreements with representatives of workers in the agencies.
2. Limits within which government administrators can negotiate with representatives of their employees.
3. The issue of exclusive collective bargaining power.
4. How the public welfare is endangered.
5. How unionized employee-management relationships affect department operational efficiency.
6. The unique position of public safety employees with respect to their alignment with organized labor and the use of the strike.

2David E. Blum: The law and public employee unions. *American County Government,* December 1966, p. 12.
3Emma Schweppe, *op. cit.,* pp. 1-2.

PRE-WORLD WAR II VIEWS

Largely as the result of the Boston police strike experience, most of the people in the early and mid-1900's viewed public employee unionism unfavorably. The conservatives of the era held that membership in a union implied the right to strike, and to strike against the government was mutiny; the very presence of unionism in public employment presented a grave challenge and danger to state sovereignty.[4] Conversely, the supporters of unionism held that unions were channels for democracy in administration and served as agents of human development.[5]

In reference to the first view, most of the opposition believed that individual employee interests were being safeguarded by public administrators and that any extension of unionism to the public sector would cause political and industrial problems. This, in turn, would create such confusion that the state itself would be threatened.[6] However, it also was recognized that the public employee needed some medium for representation. The right to organize was not challenged, only the right to affiliate with labor unions.[7] Employee organizations were acceptable, if they were confined to the civil service itself, and, if they abstained from entering into any outside affiliations.

Success of employee associations in winning public acceptance in the early days stemmed from a recognition of the widely held and fallacious notion that the state was a "model employer." Writers in the pre-World War II period specifically noted that:[8]

> . . . many department heads, who have the knowledge, lack the vision; and, what is still more lamentable, many who have the knowledge and the vision fail to possess the courage to put across the proper programs for employment.

---

[4]William Dudley Foulke: Labor unions in the civil service. *Good Government,* Vol. XXXV, 1918, p. 120.

[5]Ordway Tead: Labor unions in a democratic state. *Good Government,* Vol. 35, 1918, p. 133.

[6]Frank M. Stewart: *The National Civil Service League.* Austin, The University of Texas, 1929, p. 225.

[7]Raymond B. Fosdick: *American Police Systems.* New York, The Century Company, 1921, pp. 320-321.

[8]Emma Schweppe, *op. cit.,* p. 3.

POST-WORLD WAR II OPPOSITION

Current opposition arguments regarding public employee unionism basically remain unchanged; today it is the long-held view that the government worker's position is a unique one wherein employment conditions make unionism unnecessary. Just employment conditions are assured because the law requires "fair treatment" of employees by superiors. This reasoning continues largely as an advancement of the "model employer" concept couched in civil service law guarantees. Its validity remains highly questionable.

Those opposed to unionism also contend that the means for improving public working conditions are available through the exercise of the franchise—employees as individual citizens—and through their local employee associations. Actually, they say that the latter capability for exerting political power gives the public employee an advantage over the industrial worker who is confined to the economic sphere of influence. Therefore, if governmental authority were to sanction public employee unionism it would assist in establishing an unfair relationship between conditions of public and private employment and would discriminate in favor of union labor.[9] Thus, public employee unionism is both unnecessary and undesirable.

Additional hazards of unionism put forth by opponents include the loss of government neutrality, inordinate political power for employees, and the collapse of internal departmental discipline. They also claim that trade union practice in employee-management relations in public agencies is illegal.

The National Institute of Municipal Law Officers is a leader among those supporting this last view. At issue is whether public administrators have the authority to enter into collective bargaining agreements with representatives of employees. Opponents of unionism have held that the public officer (administrator), in the absence of express constitutional charter or legislative authorization, is without power to do so.[10] The doctrine of limited governmental powers under state constitutions and municipal charters is thus applied.

9*Ibid.*, p. 4.
10*Ibid.*, p. 6.

Viewing the issue from another point of view, opponents arrive at a similar conclusion regarding the legality of collective bargaining itself. The determination of policy, arrived at through agreements between the public officer and union representatives, is viewed as unlawful delegation of power to a private organization —the labor union. It is held that, under collective bargaining, the public employee is represented by "outside" labor agents who, in turn, receive direction from the even further removed leaders of a national union. This argument thus follows the logic that all policy must be determined in accordance with law; all money must be paid out in pursuance of legislative appropriations, and all personnel determinations must be made in terms of the civil service law as well as the rules and regulations of the departments.[11] The view that, in the absence of statutory prohibition, the public officer's discretionary powers open the process of collective bargaining to his use in disregarded. This attitude is succinctly stated as follows:[12]

> The law and regulations cover employer and employee relations in government and these contracts are merely an attempt to parallel a different rule than that provided by law.

Alleged illegality of collective bargaining agreements is based upon still another consideration. It is argued that genuine collective bargaining rests upon the prerequisite of the employees' freedom to refuse collectively to contract along with the right to strike. In other words, the right to bargain collectively carries the correlative right to strike. When this right is granted, the wheels of government can come to a grinding halt. Strike action is then an act of revolution. The possession of this right distinguishes private workers from those in public employment; the sanction is permissible to the former, but an act of mutiny in the hands of the latter.[13] Absolutely deprived of the right to strike, the public employee is logically without an adequate sanction essential to genuine collective bargaining. Thus, no useful func-

[11]*Ibid.*, p. 7.

[12]*Municipalities and the Law in Action*. Washington, D. C., The National Institute of Municipal Law Officers, 1941, p. 235.

[13]Emma Schweppe, *op. cit.*, p. 8.

tion can be served by affiliation with organized labor when genuine collective bargaining is precluded.[14]

As regards police unions specifically, they have been labeled programs of negation by the overwhelming majority of police administrators.[15] One such administrator[16] contends that past practices by union organizers and leaders relative to the enrollment of police officers have implanted fear in the mind of the public of the possibility of "self-perpetuating labor dictatorships" and "sympathy" or protest walkouts.[17] The remaining arguments advanced against police unions largely echo those applied to all public employees, with special emphasis upon the distinction between "public employees" and "public officers."

Today, the right of municipal employees, generally, to form organizations for their mutual benefit and to affiliate with labor unions is legally and professionally recognized and is becoming more and more publicly acceptable. However, one exception persists—union membership on the part of municipal police officers. Some authorities even contend that "the great majority of pro-union authorities would explicitly exclude the police from such membership."[18]

Prohibitions and restrictions affecting membership in police unions come in the form of state statutes, court rulings, attorney generals' opinions, city charter provisions, civil service regulations, decisions of the mayor and city council or other officials of the city government (administrative rulings), or unexpressed but well-understood policy within the police department itself.[19] Because of a definite lack of a substantial number of court decisions and statutory laws, the most common guides are the opinions of attorney generals and city attorneys.

A final and major argument offered against unionization of policemen is that such action prevents the police field from ever becoming professionalized. To the dedicated police officer, this

[14]*Ibid.*
[15]Roy E. Hollady: Police unions—programs of negation. *Police,* November-December 1961, p. 63.
[16]*Ibid.*
[17]*New York Times,* December 30, 1958.
[18]Roy E. Hollady, *op. cit.,* p. 66.
[19]*Ibid.*

probably is the strongest argument because the trade union movement traditionally represents both the unskilled and craft skills of the blue-collar variety. He finds no unions of medical doctors or attorneys. While he finds teachers' unions, a broad gamut of argument can be introduced as to the affect this has had upon professionalization of the teaching profession.

That law enforcement officers have no special professional status from the union perspective is brought home rather vividly in a statement by a Teamster official which was made before a hearing committee in Lewiston, Idaho on April 15, 1970. He said the following:[20]

> Affiliation certainly has no more bearing on a law officer than a milk man, bread man, freight peddler, garbage collector, office worker, station attendant, food processor, warehouseman or a construction worker. Each have their place in today's society and collective bargaining in labor is only a tool to correlate the welfare of citizens of any community; being equal to their church . . .

The modern, progressive police officer probably experiences difficulty in "buying" this line of reasoning.

POST-WORLD WAR II ADVOCATES

On the other hand, the supporters of public employee unionism claim that it is desirable for all institutions of a democratic state to reflect democratic practices. A proponent, shortly after the turn of the century, identified free unions with this democratic philosophy:[21]

> A democratic organization is one which deliberately grants representation and equal power to different parties at interest in the carrying on of that organization. . . . Where there are different parties at interest . . . representation of these parties is essential to full knowledge and to active cooperation in the conduct of the enterprise . . .

Under this theory, autocratic administrative practices are viewed as a danger to the democratic state.[22] Advocates of public

20Affidavit, Evett Byers, Secretary-Treasurer, Teamsters Union Local 551, City of Lewiston, State of Idaho, April 15, 1970.

21Ordway Tead, *op. cit.*, p. 135.

22Emma Schweppe, *op. cit.*, p. 12.

employee unionism argue that free and strong unions furnish employee representation which serves as a necessary internal check against bureaucratic power usurpations.

Is this argument valid when applied to police agencies? Where democratic administrative processes are accepted as desirable and autocratic practice condemned, the semi-military organization controlling the municipal public safety departments comes sharply into focus. Thus, in most discussions of unionism, these departments are viewed as unique because it is generally accepted that the service rendered calls for an employee discipline which is assured only by the military approach. This means exacting rules and regulations, also, orders that flow from the top down. Unionism destroys this kind of management. Furthermore, persons who enter these services appear to willingly accept the autocracy of military management as a basic condition of their employment. They generally recognize forthright military management as essential to the operation of an effective police department. Additionally, the patrolman is the following:[23]

> . . . a policy-forming administrator in miniature, who operates beyond the scope of the usual devices for popular control. He makes and unmakes the fortunes of governmental executives and administrators, though rarely falling under the direct influence of popular will. The only control to which he is subject is the discipline of his superiors. When that weakens, or is thwarted, the last vestige of control over this mighty atom of law enforcement disappears.

On the other hand, advocates of unionism contend that this autocratic management has neither safeguarded the public interest nor precluded the formation of public employee organizations. Actually they say existing autocratic management has facilitated political control of these public safety departments. They point out instances of administrative mismanagement and gross scandals throughout the country where military organization and politically subservient superior officers have only served to facilitate the political use of these departments.

It is further argued by the advocates that an internal check

---

[23]Bruce Smith: *Police Systems in the United States.* New York, Harper and Brothers, 1940, p. 21.

against the special interests of those in control is vitally needed. They claim that the channels which strong internal unions would establish could bring the facts to public notice.

Proponents of unionism also consider independent rank-and-file strength (the natural result of unionism) of paramount importance because commanding officers for public safety departments are selected from the ranks. Advancement through the ranks, regardless of the merit system, rests heavily upon superior officer evaluations of a candidate's fitness. Politically amenable individuals have tended to become the politically favored ones.[24] Unquestioning acceptance of orders down the line and cooperation in facilitating the political use of the department have been rewarded more frequently than has effective police work.[25] One writer contends that the results of internal promotion are clear:[26]

> . . . common interests, comradeship, and close association tend to weld them all in one body, the tone of which forces itself irresistibly on every recruit.

Another writer has phrased it as follows:[27]

> The fraternity of the star and the shield with the nightstick-rampant and the gun couchant on a field of blue, is a tightly knit one. United we stand, and divided we fall—or at least stumble—is the recorded motto of the cops.

The friends of unionism thus use this approach to support their contention that independent unions affiliated with organized labor would allow the majority of police employees to more readily support more effective police work and act as a deterrent to the racketeering minority often found in a police department.

Protagonists also call attention to the fact that the semi-military organization and its autocracy have not prevented the establishment of strong, quasi-union intraservice associations, some of which are affiliated with organized labor while others are aligned with public service associations on a city and/or statewide

---

[24]Emma Schweppe, *op. cit.,* p. 14.

[25]*Ibid.*

[26]*The Police Problem in New York City.* New York, The Bureau of City Betterment of the Citizens Union of the City of New York, November 1906, p. 8.

[27]Emanuel H. Lavine: *Cheese It—The Cops.* New York, Vanguard Press, 1936, p. 21.

basis. They characterize these associations as almost exclusively
political pressure groups, often aligning themselves with or being
captured by machine politicians.[28] Advocates of police unions
claim that these associations have been impotent as channels for
real consultation and negotiation.

In connection with the contention that unionism jeopardizes
the neutrality essential to a police department, advocates generally
respond by questioning the neutrality resulting from nonunion
affiliation. Realistically, they point out, the factors contributing
to or destroying police neutrality are the basic employment conditions in the public safety department. Normally, police policy
is the city administrator's policy.[29] Neither unionized nor non-
unionized police have displayed conspicuous neutrality in their
involvement with strikes throughout the country. However, most
complaints against the lack of police neutrality have come from
organized labor, although most of the men on the force are drawn
from the labor socioeconomic element and have expressed a
natural sympathy for the striker.[30]

On the issue of the legal competence of municipalities to enter
collective bargaining agreements, the advocates argue pragmatic-
ally. The power to enter into collective agreements is viewed
as fair and necessarily implied in the power delegated to responsible public officers; and, in turn, essential to the attain-
ment of the very purpose for which the municipal corporation
exists. Additionally, municipalities have previously entered into
legally binding collective bargaining agreements.[31] Friends of the
movement argue that administrative tolerance or the encourage-
ment of unions in the public service does not come from legal
competence anyway; rather, it is entirely a matter of public policy.
In a 1944 decision, the Circuit Court of Baltimore issued the
following statement regarding the legal status of labor contracts
in the field of government employment:[32]

28Emma Schweppe, *op. cit.*, p. 15.

29*Ibid.*, p. 16.

30T. S. Williamson and Herbert Harris: *Trends in Collective Bargaining.* New
York, Twentieth Century Fund, 1945, p. 193.

31Emma Schweppe, *op. cit.*, p. 18.

32*Ibid.*, p. 21.

It does not follow that every agreement with a labor union by municipal officers is unlawful. No law forbids the organization of city employees into an association; nor denies to such association the privilege of fair hearing in the matter of working conditions and term of employment. Agreement on a fixed policy for a reasonable period in regard to wages, hours, etc., may promote stability and regularity. But the preferential and exclusive features common to labor union contracts in the field of government must be altogether avoided; the right to hire others, and to fire union members must be preserved, as well as the right to hear and consider the grievances of other than union members. There must be no strike; and no closed shop.

In a subsequent decision sustaining a voluntary check-off plan, the Baltimore court held that collective dealings "have come to stay and must be regarded as an accomplished fact of modern industrial life."[33] Government must of necessity enter a competitive labor market. Through specific city ordinances, some municipalities have made provision for employee negotiations or have given city employees permission to do so. Examples are Bloomington, Illinois; Pontiac, Michigan; Detroit; Cleveland; Philadelphia; Reading, Pennsylvania; and Fairmont, West Virginia.[34]

WHY POLICEMEN JOIN UNIONS

From the above discussion we see that the police clearly are a case in point for the common argument given for unionization and the assertion of demands for collective bargaining rights by a class of workers. This occurs when police employees experience a relative decline in economic status in relationship to other occupations or industries. Policemen accept their impotent position in determining wages and working conditions only during times of general police opulence.

Since 1938, the Bureau of Labor Statistics has maintained salary data on policemen in cities of 100,000 population or over. These data cover two-thirds of all policemen in the United States. The bureau's reports reveal that between 1939 and 1950, police salaries increased 52 percent; but, during the same period, the

[33]*Ibid.*
[34]Charles S. Rhyme: *Labor Unions and Municipal Employee Law.* Washington, D. C., National Institute of Municipal Law Officers, 1946, pp. 426-436, 461-524.

average annual salary of federal employees increased 83 percent; municipal transit operating employees salaries increased 110 percent; and the consumer price index rose by 69 percent.[35] Little police union organization or collective bargaining occurred during this period, but this can be attributed to adverse legal and public opinion rather than police acquiescence.

⎯Between 1951 and 1961, policemen's salaries increased 56.9 percent which was better than the factory production worker's hourly raise of 50 percent and the factory production worker's weekly raise of 48.1 percent. The increase also was better than the federal employee's average annual salary raise of 54.1 percent, and a similar raise for municipal transit operating employees. Only urban school teachers did better with a 59 percent increase during the period.[36] The period exhibited no definite move toward police unionization.

Police increasingly turned to unions between 1961 and 1966 to achieve collective action for higher wages. During this period, policemen's salaries increased only 18.1 percent; municipal transit operating employees' salaries advanced 35 percent; federal employees' annual average salaries improved by 23 percent; and factory production workers' weekly wages rose 18.5 percent. However, policemen did better than classroom teachers, whose salaries increased only 12.1 percent.[37] This also was a time when legal and political restrictions were easing. The liberalization of public opinion was exemplified in a 1967 Gallup Poll which revealed that six out of ten persons interviewed believed that police should be permitted to join unions.[38]

Court opinions and legislation more favorable to police unionization were forthcoming. A Wisconsin Court ruled in 1966 that police membership in the AFSCME was permissible.[39] In a later case, the unanimous ruling of the Eighth U. S. Circuit Court of Appeals held, "union membership is protected by the right of

[35]Arthur M. Sackley: Trends in police and fire salaries. *Monthly Labor Review*, Vol. 88, February 1965, p. 160.

[36]*Ibid.*, p. 161.

[37]*Ibid.*

[38]Gallup Poll on police unions. *New York Times*, January 12, 1967, p. 52.

[39]Wisconsin court permits police union. *Public Employee*, November 1966, p. 10.

association under the First and Fourteenth Amendments."[40] Finally, by 1967, 17 states had enacted "little Wagner Acts" for public employees, including the police.[41]

When the wage rates of specific cities are examined rather than the results of general salary surveys, the correlation between police unrest and economic status becomes more uncertain. Of the ten top-paying cities with populations of over 500,000, San Francisco, Chicago, Los Angeles, San Diego, Seattle, and Houston have experienced little or no police unionization or collective bargaining. Detroit, Cleveland, Philadelphia, and New York are ranked third, seventh, eighth, and ninth, respectively, in the ten top-paying cities; all have experienced police unrest and unionization while the lowest paying cities in this category (San Antonio, Memphis, Kansas City, Atlanta, and Boston) have not.

Without doubt, the general economic status of policemen throughout the nation is deplorable. In 1968, the U. S. Bureau of Labor Statistics reported that the average metropolitan policeman's salary was $7,500 (by 1970, this had risen to $9,400), some 33 percent less than is needed by a family of four to live in a large city.[42] Clearly then, inadequate salaries for police and increasing unionization are only a partial cause-effect relationship. Other significant factors include: (1) declining status of policemen, (2) changing requirements of the job, and (3) failure of police agencies themselves to move forward toward realistic professionalization.

Today's policemen now find themselves in a situation considerably changed from that of 50 years ago. Then, policemen "had an income higher than other trades and there were more applicants than jobs."[43] One researcher who studied the New York City Police Department concluded:[44]

40SCME v. North Platte, Nebraska. *AFL-CIO News*, January 4, 1969, p. 3.

41Kurt Hanslowe: *The Emerging Law of Labor Relations in Public Employment*, Institute of Labor and Industrial Relations Paperback No. 4. Ithaca, New York, Cayuga Press, 1967, p. 55.

42M. W. Aussieker, Jr., *op. cit.*, p. 8.

43Seymour M. Lipset: Why police hate liberals and vice-versa. *Atlantic Monthly*, March 1969, p. 79.

44*Ibid.*, pp. 79-80.

During the depression the department was able to recruit from a population which included many unemployed or low paid college graduates . . . As general economic conditions have improved, however, the job of police officer has become less attractive to college graduates.

In surveys of police opinion in Chicago, Boston, and Washington, reports indicate that 59 percent believe that the prestige of police work is lower than it was twenty years ago.[45] An Oakland study revealed that when policemen were asked to rank their most serious problems, the category most frequently selected was "lack of respect for the police." Of the 282 policemen who rated the prestige of police work, 70 percent ranked it only fair to poor.[46] Finally, studies of police opinion have indicated that some policemen even conceal their occupations from their neighbors because many people do not like to associate with them. This bears out the Lipset contention that, "the relative socio-economic status of policemen has worsened over time."[47]

In 1968, the New York City police rejected the best economic contract ever presented to policemen. The causes for this rejection were believed by police department officials to be social rather than economic. "Policemen are feeling their muscle all over the country. They want to be special. They want status," said one official.[48] Another replied:[49]

I think it's really a general frustration that the police are feeling toward the establishment. They feel they are not getting the kind of recognition and respect they are entitled to—from either the community or the administration.

Such reaction is related to the youth of the average policeman, whose age is approximately 27 or 28 years. "They are turning their backs on material things and going after other things—ego things.[50]

[45]Jerome Skolnick: *Justice Without Trial.* New York, John Wiley & Sons, 1966, p. 53.

[46]*Ibid.,* p. 75.

[47]Seymour M. Lipset, *op. cit.,* p. 79.

[48]Sylvan Fox: Why policemen are unhappy. *New York Times,* October 24, 1968, p. 1.

[49]*Ibid.*

[50]*Ibid.*

Although the above cited article accounted for the rejection of the New York City Patrolmen's Benevolent Association contract by indicating the desire of policemen for more social status, the association president cited other reasons:[51]

> The present terms are totally unacceptable to patrolmen, who demand that the city grant pay, benefits and working conditions consistent with the risk, responsibilities and burdens that they are asked to undertake every day.

This statement reflects the opinion of thousands of policemen who believe that working conditions have substantially deteriorated over the last decade. The president continued: ". . . the job of the patrolmen is more difficult because of demonstrations, student disorders, ambushes and shooting of policemen."[52] A public relations officer of the New York Association declared at a police demonstration in front of city hall:[53]

> The police feel resentment toward city hall for what they say is the abuse they have suffered at the hands of demonstrators and others allegedly encouraged by political leaders . . . the hazards and frustrations of the job make the police feel that they are entitled to a degree of compensation way beyond that they are presently making.

Police job dissatisfaction has been encountered in cities other than New York. After interviews with policemen in Boston, Washington, and Chicago, one researcher reports:[54]

> The police believe their conditions of work have also worsened. Eighty per cent state that 'police work is more hazardous today than five years ago.' Sixty per cent believe that the way the public behaves toward the police has changed for the worse since they joined the force.

Another study by the Opinion Research Corporation on police attitudes toward their work in 12 metropolitan cities reveals that patrolmen exhibit a high level of dissatisfaction with their jobs, feel that they are misunderstood by the public, and are convinced

[51]Cassese calls contract unacceptable. *New York Times,* December 5, 1968, p. 1.
[52]*Ibid.*
[53]Police picket city hall. *New York Times,* October 19, 1968, p. 1.
[54]Seymour M. Lipset, *op. cit.,* p. 79.

that they do not get sufficient backing from the police department.[55]

Policemen attribute the worsening of their working conditions to the increasing permissiveness of society, which usually is held to be a direct result of the liberal orientation of political leaders in their respective cities. Such feelings can be expected because of the conservative attitudes of policemen. Their attitudes are rooted in their social origins, job experiences, and exposure to political interference with their work.[56]

Clearly, the dissatisfaction of policemen over their worsening socioeconomic status and their deteriorating working conditions, which they attribute to the political attitudes of their mentors, has been reflected in growing membership in police unions and nationally affiliated associations. A 1966 survey of 1,500 cities by the International City Managers Association reports that police union membership in national associations increased markedly since 1959. Seventy-three percent of cities with populations over 250,000 reported policemen with membership in these organizations. For cities of over 500,000 in population, 46 percent had officers who are members of national associations or unions. The lowest figure reported was 26 percent for cities of under 25,000 population.[57]

In summary, the relative decline in police salaries in relationship to other occupations, loss of status and prestige, the increased difficulty of police tasks attributed to social phenomena and liberal politics are causes of police unrest. These phenomena also represent needs to be fulfilled by police organizations—problems to be solved by collective bargaining. As civil service and merit systems represent earlier attempts to solve problems stemming from the growth and inefficiency of municipalities, now public agencies, police administrators, and policemen appear to be increasingly turning to collective bargaining as a means of removing the roots of police dissatisfaction.

[55]Opinion research study. *New York Times,* December 19, 1968, p. 55.
[56]Seymour M. Lipset, *op. cit.,* passim.
[57]*1966 Municipal Yearbook.* Washington, D. C., International City Managers Association, 1966, p. 40.

Chapter VIII

SUMMARY, CONCLUSIONS, AND RECOMMENDATIONS

As we have seen in the preceding discussion, the history of the trade union movement in the United States is filled with attempts to organize police departments throughout the country. Largely abortive, these efforts have, nevertheless, set the stage for today's policeman, who expresses reluctance at affiliating with the national trade union movement, while insisting on the rights of collective bargaining through his local association. This prevalent attitude, however, has not discouraged either the trade union organizers or power-oriented individuals from seeking such affiliation. The nucleus for success exists historically, sociologically, and by virtue of the existence of fraternal, social, and benefit clubs in practically every police organization of any size: organizations that often act as sub rosa collective bargaining agents.

The union movement itself evolved in the United States, almost exclusively based upon the issue of economic exploitation. After several false starts during periods of prosperity (followed by rapid decline under the pressures of depression in the nineteenth century), the union movement finally withstood the economic collapse of 1873 and, by 1878, still accounted for 50,000 members. From that point, it moved through strife and violence into the era of labor federations.

Starting with the Knights of Labor, which was founded in 1869, the bulk of unionized labor "wound up" as part of the huge American Federation of Labor (known today as the AFL-CIO). This young, aggressive, and highly capable organization spearheaded the early drives for greater worker economic parity and improved working conditions (i.e. the eight-hour day). Almost from the outset, the AFL was an organizational model which was well-suited to the requirements of the skilled trades, thereby stimulating the formation of new national unions. It acted as a stabilizer of union membership during depression periods and presented a practical operating program which has proven highly successful in winning grains on the economic front.

The AFL also has withstood the test of challenge from both within and without. In its early years, the Industrial Workers of the World (IWW) arose as a challenger (between 1890 and 1935). However, IWW, which had its strongest appeal among the migratory workers of the western states, had little success in wooing members from the AFL and never achieved a dues-paying membership in excess of 20,000 although its high turnover in membership actually meant that several hundred thousand workers passed through the organization during its existence.

From within, the challenge to the AFL was the Congress of Industrial Organizations (CIO), which splintered from the federation in 1938 over the issue of craft versus industrial organization. The success of the CIO organizing drives have become legend in trade union history. During the late 1930's, one anti-union citadel after another capitulated. These successes stemmed from a number of favorable conditions: pro-labor government administrations, the National Labor Relations Act of 1935, and a prolonged rise in business activity after 1933.

In 1955, the AFL and CIO remerged into the existing AFL-CIO, which is a federation of wholly autonomous individual unions. Its executive committee recommends action, rather than exercising any coercive power.

The AFL-CIO does not include all of the national or international unions. The Railway Brotherhoods and the United Mine Workers remain independent; and, the Teamsters, the largest union in the country, was expelled because of internal corruption. Union membership failed to follow its historic growth trends, and the peak was achieved in 1956 with an overall total of 17,500,000 or 33.4 percent of the non-agricultural employment. This total increased to 18,325,000 in 1966, but represented only 28.8 percent of non-agricultural employment.

Numerous factors account for this low percentage of trade union members. Probably, the most important consideration is a change in the structure of the civilian work force. The number of blue-collar workers, who make up the bulk of union membership, is declining while the number of nonunion white-collar workers steadily rises. Additionally, the role of government as an employer continues to grow by leaps and bounds. In traditional terms, the labor pools from which unions had drawn their membership were steadily shrinking. This meant that unions were forced to turn their attention to new fields and develop a way to effectively organize the growing number of workers who, for social rather than economic reasons, have always resisted unionism. It is for this reason that organized labor has reached into the ranks of public employees and continues to grow in strength as well as recognition.

Unionism in the public sector had its origins in the late 1800's. Although governmental agencies were small, communications poor, and unions in the private sector were embryonic, the first public employees' organizations emerged among postal employees, policemen, and teachers.

Early in the 1900's, policemen were organized in 37 cities. It was at a time when the public attitude towards police unionization was first expressed—an attitude that remains unchanged with the passing years. To the public, the policeman was the embodiment of governmental power. His alliance with the purveyors of collective bargaining seemed, to most, to be an attack upon the very foundations of the state. As a consequence, strong hostility towards the idea of police unions existed and persisted, especially those aligned with organized labor. Nevertheless, police unionism remained on the rise until the 1919 strike of policemen in Boston; following this, police unions all but disappeared for almost 25 years. However, this has not prevented the police from remaining one of the most thoroughly organized groups of American public employees. Almost every city has some kind of policemen's association, some of which trace their history back to pre-Civil War days.

Most of the police organizations originally were benevolent associations, founded early to protect the policemen and to improve his working conditions. They met little official opposition because they functioned in an inoffensive (to the police hierarchies) manner. Many were even controlled by high ranking police officials, and it appeared to be common policy to seek their ends through departmental favor or through the power of the political machine. The military-like organization of the police force made it especially easy for the department to control the association, while the power exerted by the policeman on his beat made him a valuable ally of the political machine.

This dormancy in police unionization activity was broken when the AFSCME chartered its first police local in Portsmouth, Virginia, in 1937. A few years later it took on a concerted drive for police membership, despite warnings of disaster based upon the Boston experience. By the end of 1944, the federation reported 31 police locals; and, two years later, it further reported 36 locals composed wholly of policemen and an additional 33 in which policemen were members, along with other groups of municipal employees. Despite opposition, the AFSCME police locals grew to 55 by 1947, reached 61 by 1951, but fell to 58 in 1953. This number again grew to 65 in 1959. In December of 1970, AFSCME claimed to represent approximately 11,000 policemen and sheriff's department employees. Ten thousand of these were in some 90 local police unions in 20 states. The remaining 1,000 policemen held membership in 36 locals in 15 states; each local represents these police along with other public employees. All AFSCME contracts included a no-strike clause; however, this restriction was removed in 1970.

In addition to AFSCME activity, several other affiliated AFL-CIO unions as well as unaffiliated trade unions have shown an interest in organizing the police. The most aggressive of these has been the Teamsters. Although most of the Teamster locals are in small cities, 110 out of 186 employees in the San Francisco Sheriff's Department have joined the Teamsters and are represented by them before the Board of Supervisors. The Teamsters claim to represent 2,349 policemen in a number of departments scattered across the country. Teamster charters for police locals specify that the document will be revoked if policemen strike or refuse in concert to perform their duties.

A few police locals have been established in the Service Employees International Union, which also forbids policemen from striking. While the Teamsters and Service Employees are the only nonpublic employee labor unions to organize police into locals, several other trade unions have accepted police associations as affiliates (i.e. Carpenters Local 261 in Alameda, California).

In addition to the Teamsters, AFL-CIO affiliated locals, the Service Employees, and AFSCME, the Fraternal Order of Police (FOP), founded in 1915, is currently reported to maintain some 900 locals (lodges) with a total membership of 90,000 policemen. Its president is the only full-time member of the staff. The FOP is not affiliated with the AFL-CIO and does not consider itself a labor union. It appears to be a loose confederation of low-dues, local lodges with the national encouraging autonomy for these local units.

A new all-police organization has recently been proposed. Known as the International Brotherhood of Police Officers (IBPO), it seeks an AFL-CIO charter. The avowed purpose of this organization is to unite all American policemen into a single union and win for them improved wages, hours, and working conditions. However, at the mid-winter, 1971, meeting of the AFL-CIO Executive Council, the IBPO was turned down in its request for a charter because it remains largely a paper organization.

California proved to be a microcosm of the national scene. The "issues" in the state are identical to those in other sections of the country: wages, conditions of work, increased dangers of the job, status-prestige, grievance procedures, and benefits. The approaches to solving these problems also are the same: sick-ins, sick-outs, slowdowns, strict enforcement, and the strike. Affiliations are similar: the statewide and local associations as well as membership in labor unions. In California, however, another association, somewhat reminiscent of the Fraternal Order of Police, is highly active on the scene—PORAC, the Peace Officers Research Association of California. Besides PORAC, ten other law enforcement associations exist in the state.

As of July 1, 1969, 402 cities had been incorporated in California. Of these, 62 were contracting for police services with existing law enforcement agencies. The state also had 58 sheriff's departments, 18 marshal's offices, a state highway patrol, and a state police. One hundred eighty-six police departments, 33 sheriff's departments, and 15 marshal's offices, the highway patrol, and the state police now have their own membership associations. In 1968, PORAC claimed that 140 of the municipal, 16 sheriff's, and 12 marshal's associations were affiliated with it.

California also has a provision in its Government Code, commonly referred to as the Meyers-Milias-Brown Act of 1968, which appears to partially guarantee the collective bargaining rights of public employees—that is, it requires government bodies to meet with public worker representatives. Riddled with "loopholes" and the subject of varied "interpretations," the act has resulted in a muddled relationship between employee groups and public employers. By the end of 1969, only 20 California cities had adopted ordinances granting employee salary negotiation privileges. Negotiations by police representatives were successfully accomplished in only four instances.

In December 1970, the California attorney general rendered his opinion that public employees do not have the right to strike —and, that police and firemen from other areas may be called into a city where local police or firemen are on strike.

Increasing militancy of California policemen has resulted in the introduction of a State Senate Bill ("Dills"—SB No. 333) calling for compulsory arbitration to settle labor disputes involving fire fighters and law enforcement officers. This militancy also has been loudly expressed in the three police strikes experienced in the state during 1969 and 1970.

The first police strike in California history was a joint police-fire fighter undertaking in Vallejo (population: 70,000). It continued five days, from July 17, 1969 to July 22, 1969, and took place in defiance of a court order as well as an existing state law. The PORAC organization was fully and openly involved in supporting the strikers and providing legal counsel for them. Strike settlement was achieved, based upon a compromise package as well as assurances of amnesty for the strikers and no loss of paycheck dollars for the strike period. Additionally, Vallejo withdrew its complaint from the court, thereby avoiding a judicial test of the situation. During the strike, public safety services were primarily provided by the Solano County Sheriff's Department, the California Highway Patrol, and the State Division of Forestry with state assistance costs amounting to $17,802.

Neither side could claim a "clear-cut" victory in what many throughout the state considered a "test" case. All of the strikers' announced goals were not achieved, and the city "backed down" from its original position. A significant fact emerging from the strike is that public safety employees struck in violation of California law and no penalty test was ever undertaken in the courts by the state, despite the governor's branding the strike as "illegal."

On July 11, 1970, the Antioch (population: 26,000) police apparently took their cue from Vallejo and initiated the second police strike in the history of the state. Again, the issues primarily were economic. However, the membership of Antioch policemen in PORAC also was made an issue by the city manager. This, of course, brought immediate active PORAC support for the strikers in the form of a $1,000 strike fund donation and the PORAC attorneys.

Unlike Vallejo, the Antioch authorities did not ask for county or state aid, claiming "legal complications." Instead 12-hour shifts were inaugurated for the nonstrikers: the police chief, a captain, a lieutenant, and a dispatcher. They were augmented by city officials and management personnel.

This second major police strike ended on July 14th after a compromise package was offered by the city council. The police received a 12.25 percent pay increase, amnesty, and were allowed to charge their time off to accumulated overtime.

In both of the above strikes, Central Labor Council support was sought and was forthcoming. Secondary boycotts were established by corporation yard and building trades workers, who also received amnesty and were permitted to charge their time off to leave.

Following the example of Vallejo and Antioch, Hollister's 12-member police force went out on strike November 13, 1970, leaving public safety of its 7,500 residents in the hands of the Hollister police chief. Again, the issue in this little known strike was economic. The police demanded a 10 percent pay increase, and the city offered seven and one-half percent. Law enforcement was provided by the chief and the San Benito County Sheriff's Department during the three-day strike.

The striking Hollister police returned to work on November 16th after a long session with the city manager, who warned that they would be subject to "punitive action" by the city council. Unlike Vallejo and Antioch, the police association suffered a complete defeat in Hollister.

Although newspaper accounts do not report any activity on the part of PORAC in the Hollister strike, apparently it was involved. On November 24, 1970, the local Hollister police association sent a letter of thanks to PORAC for assistance in the strike.

In the United States, the growth in local municipal employee associations from 1962 to 1968 shows an overall net increase of 50 percent. Total membership now exceeds one-quarter of a million employees. The majority of these associations represent their members in matters of wages, working conditions, and the like. They also participate in legislative activities. Sixty-three percent of the local associations (representing 85% of the members) perform both functions.

Similarly, the representation of police officers by organized labor-oriented bodies is increasing. The number of organized cities increased by 5 percent between 1966 and 1969. The Fraternal Order of Police still leads in the number of representative bodies, but the AFSCME is making significant gains. Representation by the AFSCME increased 97 percent between 1966 and 1969. However, it is of interest to note that in an August 1971 survey of 1,258 San Francisco policemen, 55 percent expressed the opinion that the Teamsters would best represent them if they decided to affiliate.

Thus, evidence exists to prove that police employee organizations are fast becoming a significant voice in the relationships between policemen and city government. Police administrators can no longer ignore the activities of these organizations. City officials must prepare to deal with them. Above all, police executives, who are caught in the middle of this controversy, must become prepared to initiate programs that will negate the need for such organizations or become equipped to cope with the consequences that may result from the intrusion of a union in the direct line of communication between the police executive and the beat patrolman.

While it appears to be generally conceded that cause exists for the average policeman to be dissatisfied with his employment conditions and the effectiveness of his local police association, police and public officials cling to a myth: the ideal of service prevents the policemen and police administrator from supporting the police union concept. This is an unrealistic position; and, despite widespread sentiment, public policy regarding the unionization of government employees is in the process of change. The laws prohibiting collective bargaining are being relaxed or abandoned in many of the leading states.

Our police are clearly a case in point for the common argument given for unionization and the assertion of demands for collective bargaining rights by a class of workers. This occurs when police employees experience a relative decline in economic status in relationship to other occupations or industries. Policemen accept their impotent position in determining wage and working conditions only during times of general police opulence.

Thus, the relative decline in police salaries in relationship to other occupations, loss of status and prestige, and the increased difficulties of police tasks attributed to social phenomena and liberal politics are causes of police unrest. These phenomena also represent needs to be fulfilled by police organizations—problems to be solved by collective bargaining. As civil service and merit systems represent earlier attempts to solve problems stemming from the growth and inefficiency of governmental entities, now the police appear to be increasingly turning to collective bargaining as a means of removing the roots of their own dissatisfaction.

In viewing the significance of the historical and current trends in the police/association/trade union interrelationships, it is essential to bear in mind the role expected of the police in the everyday life of our type of democratic society. It is, without question, unique because of its intended dedication to "officiating," thereby assuring that the daily lives of the rest of us can be spent unmolested and in pursuit of our constitutional "guarantees." Thus, we must concede that police activity affects the lives of every citizen—either by omission or commission—largely in a way unequalled by any other vocation, profession, or business in our society. As a consequence, the public expects virtues and strengths from its policemen that it would never impose upon itself. At least, this is the fallacious image of the policeman created by the people for whom he works. Very often this imagery is known as the "ideal of service"; and, because the policeman is human, he rarely lives up to this "ideal," thereby becoming the public's object of scorn and anguished disappointment. It is this unrealistic, unnatural attitude that has completely colored the history of community relationships with its police as well as the police union movement.

The evidence accumulated in this research clearly shows that the greataest upsurge of police interest in collective bargaining and possible affiliation with the trade union movement has occurred since the Boston police strike of 1919. This has resulted primarily from several factors. Firstly, one finds an almost complete failure of governmental entities to provide equitable adjustments in police salaries and working conditions to keep pace with those advantages acquired in private industry through trade union activity. Secondly, we are undergoing a sociological upheaval (often disorderly) in this country with the result that the "officiator" (the policeman) suddenly finds himself the antagonist of noncriminal and large segments of our society, as well as ostracized by other major segments. In turn, he has experienced a drastic loss in prestige, one of the former intangibles of the job, as well as rejection by a vast segment of his peers; ergo, the policeman, like all of us, seeks acceptance and the labor unions welcome him with "open arms." Thirdly, the "older" generation of police officers has done little or nothing to advance the cause of professionalism over the past twenty years, thereby merely perpetuating an archiac, unsatisfactory method of operation in most police agencies. In this connection, it is significant to note that most policemen are under 30 years of age, and their prevalent attitudes toward their jobs have more in common with the blue-collar worker than with the approaches of "professionals."

As for labor unions, they recognize the millions of governmental employees as the last largely untapped source of membership. Organization of these workers will fatten coffers as well as strengthen the hand of labor in negotiations; the potential of secondary boycotts by persons engaged in vital public services could become a potent persuader. This might be particularly true if the public safety departments were under union jurisdiction. It should be noted that the secondary boycott was used in both Vallejo and Antioch, California, in support of police demands. Additionally, the unions are aware that they have a historic appeal to policemen because some of the first public employees' organizations emerged among policemen at the turn of the century. Further, policemen are oriented toward "organization" by the very nature of their jobs, as well as the existence of their local associations.

In considering police affiliation with national trade unions, it is interesting to note the consistent opposition that the police express toward civilian review boards because "outsiders would be interfering with them." This appears completely incompatible with the current trend toward alignment with nonpolice unions and nonpolice personnel in the executive hierarchy of the trade union movement. It could be argued that the objective of the newly proposed International Brotherhood of Police Officers is intended to largely overcome this objection to affiliation. Based upon the organization's avowed purposes, however, it appears to be aimed at the creation of a pure power bloc, intended to intimidate the public into acceding to their demands. As one IBPO member put it, "Right now we're organized . . . if the mayor doesn't do what we want . . we defeat him at the polls. And someday we'll have that nationally." This researcher finds this expressed attitude to be completely antagonistic, certainly not within any "ideal of service," and an arrogant expression of contempt for public interest. It even has ominous overtones in context with maintaining any semblance of a free democratic state.

Conversely, recognizing the earlier-posed, unique position of policemen in our society, the attitude of trade unionism, as expressed by one of its officials," . . . affiliation has no more bearing on a law officer than on a . . . garbage collector . . ." is equally unacceptable.

Thus, based upon the information gathered in this research,

a number of specific conclusions relative to police unionism can be offered:

1. It is fallacious reasoning on the part of policemen to join common cause with firemen because, other than the wearing of a uniform, no similarity exists between suppressing fires and enforcing the law.
2. Considering that its known objectives are largely confined to the economic sphere, affiliation with the existing trade union movement is not compatible with the evolution of police professionalism.
3. Police officers should be given official representation (through federal and state legislation) in the formulation of salaries, working conditions, and benefits affecting them which would provide more formal recognition of the local associations.
4. The use of the strike or concerted action to prevent the normal operation of a police agency is unacceptable because of the great jeopardy to the community. Federal and state legislation forbidding such action should be reinforced and enforced.
5. In view of the two preceding conclusions, it appears esssential—where salaries, working conditions, and benefits become the subject of dispute—that compulsory third-party arbitration must also be provided. This places urgent emphasis upon developing a reasonable means for utilizing the abilities, integrity, and neutrality of the arbiter.
6. Most local police associations appear anxious to affiliate at the statewide and national levels. Such affiliation should be on a professional organizational basis (i.e. the Bar Association) with a purpose not only of introducing equity in economic interests, but standards for training, promotion, executive position, and operation.
7. Responsible public officials appear to be completely unqualified to appropriately arbitrate police labor disputes. Thus, they must equip themselves with the necessary background knowledge and develop practical plans for any eventuality in this area.

Finally, this research has illustrated, almost beyond all else, the glaring lack of information concerning current police unionization activity throughout the country. This information is essential if a full picture is to be presented for use by the public, public officials, policemen, and even labor leaders. It appears that everyone concerned has reached a crossroad in public employment policies, including the public safety organizations. If intelligent decisions are made by all concerned, the "facts" must be available to them. Therefore, these writers recommend that this study serve as a basis for a government-funded, in-depth research of the subject field with the objective of publishing a single "source book" in order to replace emotional rhetoric with pragmatic data.

APPENDICES

Appendix A

Amendment No. 35

REMOVAL OF STRIKE RESTRICTIONS FOR LAW ENFORCEMENT OFFICERS

BE IT RESOLVED:

That the International Constitution, Article VIII, Section 18, be deleted.

AND BE IT FURTHER RESOLVED:

That the International Constitution, Article VIII, is amended by appropriately renumbering the present Section 19 and all succeeding sections.

AND BE IT FURTHER RESOLVED:

That the International Constitution, Appendix A, is amended as follows:

I, _____, pledge upon my honor to observe faithfully the constitution and laws of the United States of America (substitute where inapplicable), of the American Federation of Labor and Congress of Industrial Organizations, of the American Federation of State, County and Municipal Employees, and of Local Union Number _____. I will cherish, protect and exercise the freedom these laws provide. I solemnly promise to perform faithfully all the duties assigned to me and do all in my power to exalt and promote the principles of trade union democracy and the public service as a career.

[(For use only by local unions whose members are police or other law enforcement officers.)

I hereby reaffirm the obligation I have taken as a law enforcement officer.]

AND BE IT FURTHER RESOLVED:

That Article X, of Appendix C, be deleted.

SUBMITTED BY: JERRY WURF, INTERNATIONAL PRESIDENT

AGREEMENT
Between
MULTNOMAH COUNTY, OREGON
and
MULTNOMAH COUNTY POLICE UNION
LOCAL 117, AFSCME, AFL-CIO

PREAMBLE

This Agreement is entered into by Multnomah County, Oregon, hereinafter referred to as the County, and Local 117 of the American Federation of State, County, and Municipal Employees, AFL-CIO, hereinafter referred to as the Union.

The purpose of this Agreement is to set forth those matters pertaining to rates of pay, hours of work, fringe benefits, and other matters pertaining to employment.

The parties agree as follows:

ARTICLE I

Recognition

The County recognizes the Union as the sole and exclusive bargaining agent for the purpose of establishing salaries, wages, hours, and other conditions of employment for all of its employees within the Department of Public Safety eligible to participate in the 1967 representation election, and which designated Local 117 as their collective bargaining agent.

ARTICLE II

Check Off

1. The County agrees to deduct the Union membership dues once each month from the pay of those employees who individually request, in writing, that such deductions be made. The amounts to be deducted shall be certified to the County by the Treasurer of the

Union, and the aggregate deductions of all employees shall be remitted, together with an itemized statement to the Treasurer of the Union by the first day of the succeeding month after such deductions are made.

2. The County agrees to furnish the Union each month a listing of all new employees hired during the month and of all employees who terminated during the month. Such listing shall contain the names of the employees, along with their job classifications, work locations, and home addresses.

ARTICLE III

Hours of Work

1. *Regular Hours.* The regular hours of work each day shall be consecutive except for interruptions for lunch periods.

2. *Work Week.* The work week shall consist of five (5) consecutive days—Monday through Friday inclusive—except for employees in continuous operations, discussed below.

3. *Work Day.* The work day shall consist of the current prevailing consecutive hours of work now scheduled. All employees shall be scheduled to work on a regular work shift, and each shift shall have regular starting and quiting times.

4. *Work Schedules.* Work schedules showing the employee's shift, workdays, and hours shall be posted on all department bulletin boards at all times. Except for emergency situations and during the duration of the emergency, work schedules for any work shall not be changed unless the changes are posted for ten (10) days.

5. *Continuous Operations.* Employees engaged in continuous operations are defined as being any employee or group of employees engaged in an operation for which there is regularly scheduled work for twenty-four (24) hours a day, seven days a week. The work for employees engaged in continuous operations shall consist of five (5) consecutive eight (8) hour days.

6. *Rest Periods.* All employees' work schedules shall provide for a fifteen (15) minute rest period during each one-half (1/2) shift. Rest periods shall be scheduled at the middle of each one-half (1/2) shift whenever practicable. Employees who, for any reason, work beyond their regular quitting time into the next shift shall receive a fifteen (15) minute rest period before they start to work on the next succeeding shift, when it is anticipated the overtime is expected to extend

a minimum of one and one-half (1½) hours. In addition, they shall be granted the regular rest period that occurs during the shift.

7. *Meal Periods.* All employees shall be granted a lunch period during each work shift. The County shall permit any employee who is requested to and does work two (2) hours beyond his regular quitting time, time off for his meal. Whenever practicable, meal periods shall be scheduled in the middle of the shift.

ARTICLE IV
Holidays

1. *Holidays.* The following days shall be recognized and observed as paid holidays:

> Any day the President of the United States and/or
> the Governor of Oregon declares a holiday
> New Year's Day (January 1)
> Lincoln's Birthday (1st Monday in February)
> Washington's Birthday (3rd Monday in February)
> Memorial Day (last Monday in May)
> Independence Day (July 4)
> Labor Day (1st Monday in September)
> Veterans' Day (1970—Wednesday, November 11)
> (1971 and thereafter, 4th Monday in October)
> Thanksgiving Day (4th Thursday in November)
> Christmas Day (December 25)
> *Personal Holiday
> *The personal holiday shall be one (1) day off per
> year, available at the discretion of the employee,
> with the consent of the employer.

2. *Holiday Pay.* Eligible employees shall receive one (1) day's pay for each of the holidays listed above on which they perform no work.

3. *Week-end Holidays.* Whenever a holiday shall fall on a Sunday, the succeeding Monday shall be observed as the holiday.

4. *Holiday During Leave.* Should an employee be on authorized leave with pay when a holiday occurs, such holiday shall not be charged against such leave.

5. *Holiday Work.* If an employee works on any of the holidays listed above, he shall, in addition to his holiday pay, be paid for all hours worked at the rate of time and one-half (1½) his regular rate of pay.

For the purpose of computing overtime on holidays, a week in which a holiday occurs shall be considered a thirty-two (32) hour work week, and all work beyond thirty-two (32) hours shall be considered overtime, based upon his regular hourly rate. Should two (2) holidays occur in the same week, the work week will then be considered a twenty-four (24) hours, and all work beyond twenty-four (24) hours shall be overtime. When computing overtime, all paid leave shall be considered as time worked.

ARTICLE V

Sick Leave

1. *Accrual.* Employees shall accrue sick leave at the rate of one (1) day for each month worked, to be used in the event of his illness or illness of a member of his immediate household. Sick leave may be accrued up to a maximum of one hundred and eighty (180) days.

Absence due to sickness in excess of three (3) days must be verified by a physician's certificate at the request of the County.

2. *Death.* In addition to regular sick leave, an employee shall be granted not more than three (3) days leave of absence with payment at the regular rate of pay for working time missed during such three (3) day period in the event of death in the immediate family of the employee to make household adjustments or to attend funeral services.

3. *Immediate Family.* An employee's immediate family shall be defined as spouse, parents, children, brother, sister, grandparents, father-in-law, mother-in-law, sister-in-law, or brother-in-law. In relationships other than those set forth above, under exceptional circumstances, such leave of absence may be granted by the Chairman of the Board of County Commissioners upon request.

4. *Compensation for Sick Leave.* Upon retirement, an employee shall be paid, based on his current rate, for accumulated sick leave on the following basis: one-tenth (1/10) of one (1) day's wages for each day accumulated up to sixty (60) days, except that no compensation shall be paid for accumulated sick leave to any employee who has less than thirty (30) days accumulation; and one-fifth (1/5) days compensation for each day accumulated over sixty (60) days.

ARTICLE VI

Vacation Leave

1. *Accrual.* Employees shall accrue vacation time in accordance with the following schedule:

a. Less than seven (7) years service, five-sixths (5/6) of a work day for each month of service cumulative to twenty-five (25) work days. After one (1) year of service, an employee shall be entitled to two (2) weeks (10 days) vacation per year.

b. Seven (7) years, but less than fifteen (15) years of service, one and one-fourth (1¼) work days for each month of service cumulative to thirty (30) work days; and shall be entitled to three (3) weeks (15 days) vacation per year.

c. Fifteen (15) or more years of service, one and two-thirds (1⅔) work days for each month of service cumulative to forty days; and shall be entitled to four (4) weeks (20 work days) vacation per year.

2. *Vacation Times.* Employees shall be permitted to choose either a split or entire vacation. Vacation times shall be scheduled by the County, based primarily on the needs of efficient operations and the availability of vacation relief. Employees shall have the right to determine vacation times, but, in any case, vacation times shall be selected on the basis of seniority; however, each employee will be permitted to exercise his right of seniority only once. Sign-up for vacation shall be in weekly increments.

3. *Termination or Death.* After six (6) months of service, upon the termination of an employee for any reason, or in the event of the death of an employee, all accumulated vacation shall be paid either to the employee or his heirs, whichever the case may be.

ARTICLE VII

Other Leaves

1. *Leave of Absence.* Leaves of absence without pay for a limited period, not to exceed thirty (30) days, shall be granted for any reasonable purpose, and such leaves shall be renewed or extended for any reasonable period.

2. *Jury Duty.* Employees shall be granted leave with full pay any time they are required to report for jury duty or jury service, in lieu of jury fees. If an employee is excused or dismissed prior to noon, he shall report for work.

3. *Voting Time.* Employees shall be granted two (2) hours to vote on any election day if, due to shift scheduling, they would not be able to vote.

4. *Union Business.* Employees elected to any Union Office or

selected by the Union to do work which takes them from their employment with the County shall, at the written request of the Union, be recommended by the Board of County Commissioners to the Civil Service Commission for a leave of absence exceeding thirty (30) days. Members of the Union selected by the Union to participate in any other Union activity shall be granted a leave of absence at the request of the Union. Any employee who has been granted a leave of absence and who, for any reason, fails to return to work at the expiration of said leave of absence, shall be considered as having resigned his position with the County, and his position shall thereupon be declared vacated; except and unless the employee, prior to the expiration of his leave of absence, has made application for and has been granted an extension of said leave or has furnished evidence that he is unable to return to work by reason of sickness or physical disability.

5. *Maternity Leave.* Maternity leave, not to exceed six (6) months, shall be granted at the request of the employee. Maternity leaves may be extended or renewed for a period not to exceed six (6) months.

6. *Educational Leave.* After completing one (1) year of service, an employee, upon request, may be granted a leave of absence without pay for educational purposes at an accredited school when it is related to his employment. The period of such leave of absence shall not exceed one (1) year, but it may be renewed or extended at the request of the employee, when necessary.

One (1) year leaves of absence, with any requested extension, for educational purposes may not be provided more than once in any three (3) year period.

Employees shall also be granted leaves of absence with or without pay for educational purposes, for reasonable lengths of time, to attend conferences, seminars, briefing sessions, or other functions of a similar nature that are intended to improve or upgrade the individual's skill or professional ability, provided it does not interfere with the operation of the County.

7. *Military Service.* Any employee who is a member of the National Guard or the Military or Reserve Forces of the United States, who is ordered by the appropriate authorities to attend a prescribed training program or to perform other duties under the supervision of the United States or this State, shall be granted a leave of absence with pay up to thirty (30) days during the period of such activity. The same shall

apply to employees who serve the United States as a result of the Selective Service Act, except for disciplinary action.

8. *Peace Corps Service as Provided by Statute.* Any employee who enters the Peace Corps of the United States shall be given leave for such service as provided by Statute.

ARTICLE VIII

Severance Pay

Any employee who has completed one (1) full year of service with the County and who shall be laid off permanently as a result of causes other than dismissal, retirement, or resignation, shall receive one (1) full week's pay for each completed year of service with the Employer. Such severance pay shall be in addition to any other accrued pay to which the employee is entitled. However, should the employee be offered and refuse transfer, reclassification with the same pay scale, or retraining, his refusal shall be considered as a resignation.

ARTICLE IX

Health and Welfare

1. *Medical-Hospital.* The County agrees to pay the full cost for each employee of either available health plan, including "major medical" provisions, which coverage shall include the employee and his immediate family, i.e. wife/husband and dependent children.

2. *Life Insurance.* The County agrees to provide each employee covered by this Agreement with term life insurance in the amount of five thousand dollars ($5,000) for each employee. Upon retirement, employees with fifteen (15) years or more of service will be provided two thousand dollars ($2,000) coverage. Employees shall designate their beneficiaries.

ARTICLE X

Wages

1. *Wages and Classification Schedule.* Employees shall be compensated in accordance with the wage schedule attached to this Agreement and marked Appendix B, which is existing pay schedule. The attached Wage Schedule shall be considered a part of this Agreement.

When any position not listed on the Wage Schedule is established, the County may designate a job classification and pay rate for the position. In the event the Union does not agree that the classification and/or rate are proper, the Union shall have the right to submit the issue as a grievance at Step III of the grievance procedure. Whenever an employee, in an emergency, performs work for more than one (1) shift in a classification above that in which the employee is normally classified, the employee shall be paid for such work at the rate assigned to the higher classified work in the appropriate step according to promotional policy.

2. *Pay Periods.* The salaries and wages of employees shall be paid bi-weekly on Friday of the week following the pay period. In the event the Friday payday is a holiday, the preceding day shall be the pay-day.

3. *Hazardous or Obnoxious Work.* Employees performing hazardous or obnoxious work, not a part of their normal duties, shall be paid a premium of ten cents (10¢) per hour in addition to their regular rate of pay for all hours during which they are required to perform this type of work. This pay shall be in addition to any other rate that may apply to the job. The job classification to which this provision applies and the occasions on which this provision will apply shall be mutually agreed upon by the Union and the County. If the parties cannot agree, the matter shall be submitted as a grievance at Step III of this grievance procedure.

4. *Reporting Time.* Any employee who is scheduled to report for work and who presents himself for work as scheduled, but where work is not available for him, shall be excused from duty and paid at his regular rate for a day's work.

5. *Call-In Time.* Any employee called to work outside his regular shift shall be paid for a minimum of two (2) hours at the rate of time and one-half (1½). This includes all court appearance out of shift.

6. *Overtime.* Time and one-half (1½) the employee's regular hourly rate of pay shall be paid for work under any of the following conditions, but compensation shall not be paid twice for the same hours:

a. All authorized work performed in excess of eight (8) hours in any work day.

b. All authorized work performed in excess of forty (40) hours in any work week.

c. Overtime worked shall be considered all work performed fifteen (15) minutes after the end of a normal shift, and all time over fifteen (15) minutes shall be considered one-half (½) hour for pay purposes.

    d. All authorized work performed on Saturday (sixth day) except as excluded below shall be paid for at the rate of time and one-half (1½) the employee's regular rate.

    e. All authorized work performed on Sunday (seventh day) except as excluded below shall be paid for at the rate of two (2) times the employee's regular rate, except that double time shall not apply to a day declared a state emergency by Governor or the Chairman of the Board of County Commissioners.

7. *Exceptions.* The overtime rate specified above for Saturday and Sunday work shall not be paid employees for whom these days fall regularly within the first five (5) days of their work week. These employees shall be paid time and one-half (1½) for all work performed on the sixth (6th) and double (2) time for the seventh (7th) day except as excluded by paragraph 6.e. preceding.

8. *Distribution.* Overtime work shall be distributed as equitably as practical among employees within the same job classification in each agency, when practical.

9. *Mileage Pay.* Whenever an employee is required to work at any location other than his permanent place of reporting, he shall be paid at the rate of twelve cents (12¢) per mile from his permanent reporting place for the use of his personal transportation to and from the temporary new location. All employees shall be allowed pay from the time of reporting to their permanent reporting place, and this shall end when they return to their permanent reporting place.

10. *Specialist Pay.* In addition to the established wage rate, the County shall pay specialist pay of fifty dollars ($50.00) per month to Deputy Sheriff patrolmen personnel assigned for other than on-the-job training to Radio Dispatchers, Intelligence Section, Vice Section, Juvenile Section, Crime Against Persons Section, Crime Against Property Section, Administration, Water Patrol, Public Utility Commission Regulations, Enforcement Officer and Motorcycle Patrol. On-the-job training for these positions shall not exceed thirty (30) days, and there shall be no on-the-job training time requirements for motorcycle operators.

11. *Shift Differential Pay.* In addition to the established wage rates, the County shall pay an hourly premium of fifteen cents (15¢) to clerical employees for all hours worked on shifts beginning between

the hours of twelve (12) noon and seven (7) p.m., the hourly premium of twenty cents (20¢) to all employees for hours worked on shifts beginning between the hours of seven (7) P.M. and six (6) A.M., and an hourly premium of twenty-five (25) cents per hour for all clerical employees who are assigned to the relief shift.

12. *Non-Sworn Personnel.* The County agrees to an increase in salary for each non-sworn employee recovered by this Agreement as set forth in Schedule B of this Agreement, by reference incorporated herein. The County further agrees to contribute two (2) percent additionally toward the retirement of such personnel.

ARTICLE XI

Discipline and Discharge

1. *Discipline.* Disciplinary action or measures shall include only the following: oral reprimand, written reprimand, demotion, suspension, or discharge in writing.

Disciplinary action may be imposed upon any employee only for failing to fulfill his responsibilities as an employee. Any disciplinary action or measure imposed upon an employee may be processed as a grievance through the regular procedure. If the County has reason to reprimand an employee, it shall be done in a manner that will not embarrass the employee before other employees or the public.

2. *Discharge.* The County shall not discharge any employee without just cause. If, in any case, the County feels there is just cause for discharge, the employee involved will be suspended for fifteen (15) days. The employee and his Union representative will be notified in writing that the employee has been suspended and is subject to discharge. Such notification shall state the nature of the offense for which the employee is being discharged, in detail, specifying dates, locations, and the particular nature of the offense committed by the employee.

The Union shall have the right to take up the suspension and/or discharge as a grievance at Step III of the grievance procedure, and the matter shall be handled in accordance with this procedure through arbitration, if deemed necessary by either party.

Any employee found to be unjustly suspended or discharged shall be reinstated with full compensation for all lost time and with full restoration of all other rights and conditions of employment, unless otherwise stipulated by a court of law.

ARTICLE XII

Settlement of Disputes

1. *Grievance and Mediation Procedure.* Any grievance or dispute which may arise between the parties, including the application, meaning or interpretation of this Agreement, shall be settled in the following manner:

Step I. A Union representative, with or without the employee, may take up the grievance or dispute with the employee's immediate divisional supervisor within ten (10) working days of its occurrence; if at that time the representative is unaware of the grievance he may take it up within ten (10) working days of his knowledge of its occurrence. The divisional supervisor shall then attempt to adjust the matter and respond to the representative within three (3) working days.

Step II. If the grievance has not been settled, it may be presented in writing by the Union representative, or the Union grievance committee, to the department head within seven (7) working days after the divisional supervisor's response is due. The department head shall respond to the Union representative or the grievance committee in writing within five (5) working days.

Step III. If the grievance still remains unadjusted, it may be presented by the Union representative, or the Union grievance committee, to the Chairman of the Board of County Commissioners, or his designee(s) within seven (7) working days after the response of the department head is due. The Chairman of the Board of County Commissioners, or his designee(s) shall respond in writing to the representative, or grievance committee, within five (5) working days.

Step IV. If the grievance is still unsettled, either party may within ten (10) working days after the reply of the Chairman of the Board of County Commissioners is due, by written notice to the other, request mediation.

Step V. Mediation: The mediation proceeding shall be conducted through the Oregon State Mediation and Conciliation Service. The mediator shall be requested to begin taking evidence and testimony within fifteen (15) days after submission of the request for mediation and shall be requested to issue his decision within thirty (30) days after the conclusion of testimony and argument.

Expenses for the mediation shall be borne equally by the County and the Union. However, each party shall be responsible for compensating its own representatives and witnesses. If either party desires a verbatim recording of the proceedings, it may cause such a record to be made, providing it pays for the record and makes copies available without charge to the other party and the mediator.

2. *Stewards.* Employees selected by the Union to act as Union representatives shall be known as "stewards." The names of the employees selected as stewards, and the names of local Union representatives, State Council or International representatives who may represent employees shall be certified in writing to the County by the Union.

3. *County-Union Meetings.* The Chairman of the Board of County Commissioners, or his designee(s), shall meet at mutually convenient times with the Union Grievance Committee. All grievance committee meetings with the County shall be held during working hours, on County premises, and without loss of pay. The Union Grievance Committee shall consist of five (5) members selected by the Union.

The purposes of grievance committee meetings will be to adjust pending grievances and to discuss procedures for avoiding future grievances. In addition, the committee may discuss with the County other issues which would improve relationships between the parties. Prior notice of topics for discussion at such meetings shall be furnished by each party to the other.

4. *Processing Grievances.* Grievance Committee members may investigate and process grievance during working hours, within reasonable limits, without loss of pay.

ARTICLE XIII

General Provisions

1. *No Discrimination.* The provisions of this Agreement shall be applied equally to all employees in the bargaining unit without discrimination as to age, marital status, race, color, creed, national origin, or political affiliation. The Union shall share equally with the County the responsibility for applying the provisions of the Agreement.

All references to employees in this Agreement designate both sexes, and wherever the male gender is used it shall be construed to include male and female employees.

The County agrees not to interfere with the rights of employees to become members of the Union and there shall be no discrimination, interference, restraint, or coercion by the County, or any County representative, against any employee because of Union membership or because of any employee in an official capacity on behalf of the Union, or for any other cause, provided such activity or other cause does not interfere with the effectiveness and efficiency of County operations in serving and carrying out its responsibility to the Public.

2. *Bulletin Boards.* The County agrees to furnish and maintain suitable bulletin boards in convenient places in each work area to be used by the Union. The Union shall limit its postings of notices and bulletins to such bulletin boards.

3. *Visits by Union Representatives.* The County agrees that accredited representatives of the American Federation of State, County and Municipal Employees, AFL-CIO, whether local Union representatives, district council representatives, or international representatives, upon reasonable and proper introduction, shall have reasonable access to the premises of the County at any time during working hours to conduct Union business.

4. *Existing Conditions.* All existing and future work rules and benefits shall be subject to mutual agreement before becoming effective. Changes in all such existing conditions shall be negotiated with the Union. Whenever any conditions are changed or new conditions are established, they shall be posted promiently on all bulletin boards for a period of ten (10) consecutive days. The Union and the County will jointly participate in making recommendations concerning all new classifications to the Civil Service Commission.

5. *Rules.* The County agrees to furnish each employee in the bargaining unit with a copy of all existing work rules thirty (30) days after they become effective. New employees shall be provided a copy of the rules at the time of hire.

Any unresolved complaint as to the reasonableness of any new or existing rule, or any complaint involving discrimination in the application of new or existing rules, shall be resolved through the grievance procedure.

6. *Uniforms and Protective Clothing.* If an employee is required to wear a uniform, protective clothing, or any type of protective device, such uniform, unless normally provided by employee according to industrial practices, protective clothing, or protective device shall be furnished to the employee by the County; the cost of maintaining the uniform or protective clothing or device, including initial tailoring, shall be paid by the County. Clothing and other devices other than uniforms, protective clothing and devices now provided, shall continue

to be provided and shall be uniformly provided by job classification by the County.

7. *Seniority.* This shall be defined as the total length of unbroken service within the Department of Public Safety.

ARTICLE XIV

Workmen's Compensation

1. All County employees will be insured under the provisions of the Oregon State Workmen's Compensation Act for injuries received while at work for the County.

2. The County shall supplement the amount received by the employee from the State Workmen's Compensation for on-the-job injuries in an amount to ensure the injured employee one hundred per cent (100%) of his bi-weekly net take-home pay, subject to the following conditions:

   a. The day of injury shall be considered a work day, and the employee will receive his normal salary for that day.

   b. The day following the day of injury and the next succeeding day shall be charged as sick leave, unless the employee is hospitalized (treatment in hospital, not outpatient care). In the event of hospitalization for more than seven (7) days due to injury, or absence for fourteen (14) or more days due to injury, the employee will receive supplemental payments for each day of absence for which he receives State Workmen's Compensation.

   c. If the absence due to injury is for a period of six (6) months or more, the injured employee must present to the Board of County Commissioners a physician's statement setting forth the nature of the injuries, current conditions, and anticipated length of absence or date of return. Based upon circumstances, it shall be at the discretion of the Board whether or not to continue supplemental payments.

ARTICLE XV

Liability Insurance

The County shall purchase liability insurance in such amounts and containing such terms and conditions as are necessary for the protection of all deputy sheriffs, deputy under-sheriffs, and all other persons covered by this Agreement against claims against them incurred in or arising out of the performance of their official duties. The premiums for such insurance shall be paid by the County.

ARTICLE XVI

Savings Clause

Should any Article, Section, or portion thereof, of this Agreement be held unlawful and unenforceable by any court of competent jurisdiction, such decision of the court shall apply only to the specific Article, Section, or portion thereof, directly specified in the decisions; upon the issuance of such a decision, the parties agree immediately to negotiate a substitute, if possible, for the invalidated Article, Section, or portion thereof.

ARTICLE XVII

Termination

1. This Agreement shall be effective as of the 1st day of July, 1970, and shall remain in full force and effect until the 30th of June, 1971. It shall be automatically renewed from year to year thereafter unless either party shall notify the other, in writing, not later than January 1, 1971, that it wishes to modify this Agreement for any reason, including provisions for union security. Notification shall include the substance of the modification and the language with which such desired modifications are to be expressed. In the event that such notice is given, negotiations shall begin not later than January 15, 1971. This Agreement shall remain in full force and effect during the period of negotiations.

2. The salary schedule adopted herein is subject to the following provisions: If the Portland, Oregon, Police receive an increase over that salary paid to County Police, negotiations shall be reopened with the guarantee that salaries will be no lower than those paid to Portland Police. It is intended that should the Portland Police receive a retroactive increase greater than the salary paid to County Police, the County Police will be paid a similar amount.

IN WITNESS WHEREOF, the Parties hereto have set their hand this July 23, 1970.

MULTNOMAH COUNTY
POLICE UNION LOCAL 117

John P. Dow, President
Robert G. Skipper, Vice President
Walter Hawkins, Secretary-Treasurer

MULTNOMAH COUNTY, OREGON
BOARD OF COUNTY COMMISSIONERS

M. James Gleason, Chairman
L. W. Aylsworth, Commissioner
David Eccles, Commissioner
Donald E. Clark, Commissioner
Mel Gordon, Commissioner

Classification and Salary Plan

Sworn Personnel	Job Group		
Chief	80	Corrections Officers	74
Captain	79	Corrections Officer Supervisor	76
Lieutenant	78	Fire Maintenance Engineer	60
Sergeant	77	Identification Clerk	73
Detective	77	Jail Administrator	18
ID Technician	76	Jail Counselor	93
Deputy Patrolman	75	Jail Steward	11
		Laundry Supervisor	10
Non-Sworn Personnel		Legal Stenographer	73
Accounting Clerk	73	Maintenance Carpenter	58
Administrative Assistant	91	Police Recording Clerk 1	71
Assistant Jail Counselor	92	Police Recording Clerk 2	72
Citizen's Affairs Coordinator	15	Steno Clerk 1	71
Clerk Typist I	70	Steno Clerk 2	72
		Stores Clerk	72

Job Group	Step 1	Step 2	Step 3	Step 4	Step 5	Step 6
10	$ 659	682	704	726	747	770
11	717	741	765	790	814	839
15	963	996	1,029	1,063	1,096	1,129
18	1,186	1,230	1,271	1,312	1,353	1,393
70				444	472	501
71				471	502	533
72	529	547	564	582	600	617
73	569	587	606	625	643	662
74	659	682	704	726	747	770
75	800	822	844	866	888	910
76	856	880	904	923	952	976
77	912	938	964	990	1,016	1,042
78	1,035	1,063	1,091	1,119	1,147	1,175
79	1,112	1,142	1,172	1,202	1,232	1,262
91	781	806	831	850	881	906
92	847	874	901	928	955	985
93	1,008	1,040	1,071	1,102	1,133	1,164

Appendix C

AGREEMENT BETWEEN TEAMSTERS UNION LOCAL 695 AND THE COUNTY OF WAUKESHA, WISCONSIN (SHERIFF'S DEPARTMENT)

AGREEMENT

This agreement, made and entered into at the City of Waukesha, Wisconsin, by and between the County of Waukesha, a municipal corporation, as municipal employer, and representatives of certain employees who are employed by the County of Waukesha in the Sheriff's Department.

It is the intent that the following agreement shall be an implementation of the provisions of Section 111.70J of the Wisconsin Statutes, consistent with that legislative authority which devolves upon the County of Waukesha, the statutes and, insofar as applicable, the rules and regulations relating to or promulgated by the Civil Service Ordinance.

Both of the parties to this agreement are desirous of improving employee efficiency and quality of service to the County and the public and are desirous of reaching an understanding with respect to the employer/employee relationship which exists between them and to enter into an agreement covering rates of pay, hours of work, and conditions of employment.

ARTICLE I

Section I

Management Rights

Except as otherwise specifically provided herein, the management of the County of Waukesha and the direction of the work force, including but not limited to the right to hire, the right to promote, the right to decide job qualifications for hiring, the right to lay off for lack of work or funds, the right to abolish and/or create positions,

145

the right to make reasonable rules and regulations governing conduct and safety, and the right to determine schedules of work shall
be vested in management. Management in exercising these functions
will not discriminate against any employee because of his/her representation by the Union.

Section II

Recognition

The municipal employer recognizes Teamsters Union Local No.
695 as the exclusive bargaining representative of all law enforcement
personnel who have the power to make arrests, including Matrons,
but excluding the Sheriff, Captain, Lieutenants, and the Administrative Assistant of the Sheriff's Department who have chosen the
Union to represent them for the purposes of negotiating in relation
to wages, hours, and conditions of employment.

Section III

Existing Practices

In the interpretation of this agreement nothing shall be construed
as an existing practice unless it meets each of the following tests. It
must be:
1. Long continued.
2. Certain and uniform.
3. Consistently followed.
4. Generally known by the parties hereto.
5. Must not be in opposition to the terms and conditions of this
   contract.

ARTICLE II—CHECK OFF

Section I

The employees listed on the petition and authorization, submitted
to the employer, agree to pay to Teamsters Union Local No. 695 the
sum of seven dollars ($7.00) per month for and in consideration of
the representation which Local No. 695 will render under Section
111.70J of the Wisconsin Statutes.

Section II

The employer agrees to deduct from the wages of said employees
of the bargaining unit, as referred to in Article I, and other employees

of the Sheriff's Department, who during the life of this agreement, choose Teamsters Union Local No. 695 as their bargaining representative, the sum of seven dollars ($7.00) per month, and to remit this sum to the treasurer of Teamsters Union Local No. 695 at the end of each month.

Section III

This assignment and authorization shall be in force until terminated by the employee upon at least sixty (60) days written notice to the County prior to expiration of the current contract.

Section IV

It is expressly understood and agreed that the Union will refund to the County or to the employee involved any Union dues erroneously collected by the County and paid to the Union. The Union agrees to hold County harmless from any claims or demands arising out of the County's compliance with the provisions of this Article II.

ARTICLE III—GRIEVANCE PROCEDURE

A. *Purpose*

The purpose of this grievance procedure is to provide a method for quick and binding final determination of every question of interpretation and application of the provisions of this agreement, thus preventing the protracted continuation of misunderstandings which may arise from time to time concerning such questions. The purpose of the complaint procedure is to provide a method for prompt and full discussion and consideration of matters of personal irritation and concern of an employee with some aspect of employment.

B. *Definitions*

1. A *grievance* is defined to be an issue concerning the interpretation or application of provisions of this agreement or compliance therewith.
2. A *complaint* is any matter of dissatisfaction with any aspect of employment which does not involve any grievance as defined above. It may be processed through the application of the first three (3) steps of the grievance procedure.
3. There shall be no retroactivity prior to the date of the filing of the written grievance or complaint, if complainant is found guilty as charged, except that in the event of a payroll error not occurring

as a result of employee negligence, corrected payment shall be
made retroactive.

C. *Procedure*

1. The employee and/or his Union representative shall attempt to
   settle the issue with the immediate supervisor.

2. If the issue is not settled, then the employee, his representative,
   and the immediate supervisor shall attempt to settle the issue with
   the department head. Such issue shall be in writing stating fully the
   details of the grievance submitted within five (5) workdays of
   step (1). The decision of the department head shall be rendered
   within five (5) workdays.

3. If a satisfactory settlement is not reached as outlined in step (2)
   either party may submit the grievance within ten (10) workdays
   to the Personnel Committee who shall hear the grievance within
   five (5) workdays after it has been received or after its recipient and
   shall render their decision within five (5) workdays.

4. If a satisfactory settlement is not reached as outlined in step (3)
   then either party may submit the grievance to the Sheriff's Grievance Committee who shall hold a hearing within five (5) workdays after receiving the grievance and render its decision within
   five (5) days after hearing the grievance.

5. If a satisfactory settlement is not reached as outlined in step (4),
   either party may request the other to submit the grievance to
   arbitration.

   a. One arbitrator to be chosen by the employer, one (1) by the
      Union and a third to be chosen by the first two (2), and he shall
      be the chairman of the board. (If the two (2) cannot agree
      on the selection of the third member, the party shall request
      the Wisconsin Employment Relations Commission to name the
      third member.) The board of arbitration shall, by a majority
      vote, make a decision on the grievance, which shall be final
      and binding on both parties. Only questions concerning the
      application or interpretation of this contract are subject to
      arbitration.

6. Each party shall bear the cost of its chosen arbitrator and the
   cost of the third arbitrator shall be shared equally by the parties.

7. *Resolution of Grievance or Complaint*
   If the grievance or complaint is not processed within the time
   limit at any step of the grievance or complaint procedure, it shall

be considered to have been resolved by previous disposition. Any time limit in the procedure may be extended by the mutual consent of the parties. A Union representative may be present at any step in the grievance and/or complaint procedure.

ARTICLE IV—GRIEVANCE COMMITTEE

Section I

The Union will give to the County in writing the names of the grievance representatives.

Section II

Employees representing the Union in the processing of a grievance shall be eligible to receive County compensation for time served as a grievance representative up to and including step (4) of the grievance procedure if occurring during the employees scheduled hours of work.

ARTICLE V—SENIORITY

Section I

Definition

Seniority shall mean the status attained by length of continuous service following the successful completion of a probationary period. The employee's continuous service date shall be retroactive to the last day the employee entered County service. This will indicate time worked excluding personal leave of absence exceeding thirty (30) days but including leave of absence granted for illness and United States Military Service.

Section II

During probationary period employees may be discharged or laid off without regard to seniority.

Section III

Application of Seniority

1. Seniority shall be applied and maintained within the Sheriff's Department.
2. Seniority shall apply to vacations, lay offs, recall from lay off, advancement (promotion) to a job or position requiring employee application and utilization of greater skill and responsibility, trans-

fer, when the need permits otherwise such personnel transactions shall be as hereafter provided.

3. *Loss of Seniority*

Employees shall lose their seniority for any of the following reasons:

a. Discharge, if not reversed.

b. Resignation.

c. Absent for two (2) consecutive scheduled workdays without notifying the County of the reason for absence and who has no legitimate reason for being absent from work, shall be considered as having resigned.

d. Unexcused failure to return to work after the expiration of a vacation period, leave of absence, or period for which workmen's compensation was paid.

e. Retirement.

f. On lay off for a continuous period of time equivalent to twenty-four (24) or more calendar months.

ARTICLE VI

Section I

Effective January 3, 1970, the classifications and salary ranges shall be as follows:

Classification	Range Steps					
	1	2	3	4	5	6
Deputy Sheriff	635	676	702	730	757	785
Assistant Process Administrator	635	676	702	730	757	785

Step 1—Starting Salary
Step 2—After Six Months
Step 3—Start of Second Year
Step 4—Start of Third Year
Step 5—Start of Fourth Year
Step 6—Start of Fifth Year

	1	2
Detective	810	836
Identification Officer	810	836
Huber Law Officer	810	836
Juvenile Officer	810	836

Sergeant	815	845
Detective Sergeant	885	905
Process Administrator	815	845
Juvenile Administrator	815	845

Step 1—Starting Salary
Step 2—Start of Second Year

	1	2	3	4	5
Jail Matron III	535	555	575	595	615
Jail Matron I	455	475	495	515	535

Step 1—Starting Salary
Step 2—After Six Months
Step 3—Start of Second Year
Step 4—Start of Third Year
Step 5—Start of Fourth Year

Employees at the maximum salary on December 31, 1969, shall have their rate of pay adjusted to the new maximum salary herein established and all other employees will have their salaries adjusted to the level stipulated in the salary schedule as will be determined by their length of service and merit.

Section II

Overtime

The normal work schedule shall be four (4) days on and two (2) days off and then five (5) days on and two (2) days off, on a rotating schedule. Eight (8) hours and fifteen (15) minutes shall constitute a normal workday.

Overtime shall be paid at the rate of time and one half (1½) the regular rate after the normal scheduled workweek, with the exception of those hours involved in compulsory training outside the normal schedule.

Section III

Compensatory Time

1. A regular full-time employee may elect to accumulate, during the calendar year, compensatory time up to a maximum of twenty-four (24) hours in lieu of pay.
2. The employee shall be paid for approved compensatory time at

time and one half (1½) for time worked in excess of twenty-four (24) hours.

3. All compensatory time accumulated by an employee during the calendar year shall be paid on the last pay period of the year.

4. The employee may use compensatory time at his discretion with the approval of the department head.

Section IV

Call In

All employees covered by this agreement shall respond to a call to work outside of their regular schedule of hours, by their department head or others designated by the department head. A minimum of two (2) hours at time and one half (1½) shall be granted to any employee who is requested to report outside his regular schedule of hours or report to work as scheduled and is sent home.

Section V

Holidays

All employees covered by this agreement shall be entitled to compensatory time off, at straight time, for the following holidays:

New Year's Day
Memorial Day
Independence Day
Labor Day
Veteran's Day
Thanksgiving Day
Christmas Day

The last scheduled one-half workday (4 hours) before Christmas Day.
The last scheduled one-half workday (4 hours) before New Year's Day.

To be eligible for holiday pay, the employee must work the last scheduled shift the day before and the day after the holiday unless regularly scheduled off on either day or has an excused absence.

Holidays not taken shall be considered as compensatory time under the twenty-four (24) hours provision of Article VI, Section 3.

All holidays accumulated by an employee during the calendar year must be taken during that calendar year or be paid for at the straight time rate on the last pay period of the year.

Section VI

Longevity Pay

Longevity pay shall mean a percentage of salary earned by the employee based on length of continuous service paid to qualifying employees in addition to their total earnings according with the following schedule. Longevity pay will be based on all earnings.

6th year	2.00% of gross earnings
7th year	2.50% of gross earnings
8th year	3.00% of gross earnings
9th year	3.50% of gross earnings
10th year	4.00% of gross earnings
11th year	4.25% of gross earnings
12th year	4.50% of gross earnings
13th year	4.75% of gross earnings
14th year	5.00% of gross earnings
15th year	5.25% of gross earnings
16th year	5.50% of gross earnings
17th year	5.75% of gross earnings
18th year	6.00% of gross earnings
19th year	6.25% of gross earnings
20th year	6.50% of gross earnings

Continuous service means uninterrupted service due to resignation or discharge and shall indicate time spent on the payroll excluding leaves of absence in excess of thirty (30) continuous days and lay offs.

Longevity Payments

1. Employees who qualify for longevity pay shall receive these payments added to their earnings.
2. Longevity payments shall be computed as follows:
   a. Employees whose anniversary dates appear within the first calendar quarter shall receive longevity pay computed from the preceding January 1.
   b. Employees whose anniversary dates appear within the second and third calendar quarter shall receive longevity pay computed from July 1.
   c. Employees whose anniversary dates appear within the fourth calendar quarter shall receive longevity pay computed from January 1 of the following year.

d. An employee terminating County employment prior to July 1 or January 1 shall receive longevity pay on a prorated basis for the amount of time served.

ARTICLE VII—LAY OFF AND RECALL

Section I

Lay off shall mean the separation of an employee from the active work force due to lack of work or funds or to the abolition of position due to changes in the organization.

Section II

The lay off of regular employees in any department shall be in inverse order of seniority in the department affected except as hereinafter provided.

Section III

Recall from Lay Off

1. The names of employees laid off through no fault of their own shall remain on the departmental call list for a period equal to twenty-four (24) calendar months from date of lay off.
2. Employees recalled from lay off shall be given maximum length of time of five (5) workdays to respond after notice has been sent by certified mail to their last known address on file with the County Personnel Administrator and five (5) workdays to resume work.
3. Employees who decline recall or who fail to respond or return to work directed within the time allowed shall be presumed to have resigned and their names are to be removed from seniority and if reemployed shall return to work as a new employee.

Section IV

Employees of a higher classification scheduled for lay off or whose job is eliminated are eligible to replace employees of a lesser classification within their department. If the employee scheduled for lay off has more service in the department than the person being replaced, the person in the position with the least service shall be displaced. Employees, whose jobs are eliminated or who by reason of greater seniority replace a lower-classified employee, shall be given the first opportunity to be restored to their original position of equal pay without being required to submit to a test. Such individuals, when offered job restoration decline to accept, shall forfeit all rights to such position.

Section V

Notice sent the employee or member of his family, directed to the employee's last address appearing on the County personnel record located in th office of the Personnel Administrator shall constitute a sufficient notice of work availability.

ARTICLE VIII—CLOTHING ALLOWANCE

The employer agrees to provide the initial allotment of clothing as required; thereafter, all employees covered by this agreement shall receive twelve dollars and fifty cents ($12.50) per month clothing allowance.

ARTICLE IX—VACATION

1. Regular full-time and regular scheduled part-time employees are eligible to earn and accrue paid vacation. The employee shall work the majority scheduled workdays during the month for which vacation credit is to accrue except for time spent on paid vacation or sick leave.
   a. *Regular Part-Time Employee*
      Any employee having successfully completed a probationary period of employment of six (6) calendar months and who is employed a minimum of forty (40) hours in each pay period of two (2) consecutive workweeks.
2. All vacation time is to be figured on a calendar year basis and all vacation time earned during the calendar year must be taken during the following year and at the discretion of the department head.
3. During the first calendar year and for each succeeding year through the ninth (9) year of continuous employment, an employee can earn one (1) day of vacation for each month of employment with a maximum of ten (10) days. Regular part-time employees earn and accrue one-half (½) vacation benefits.
4. During the tenth (10) year of continuous employment with the County and during each calendar year thereafter, an employee may earn one and one-half (1½) days of vacation for each month of employment with a maximum of fifteen (15) days per year through the nineteenth (19) year.

5. During the twentieth (20) year of continuous employment with the County and during each calendar year thereafter, an employee may earn two (2) days of vacation for each month of employment with a maximum of twenty (20) days per year.
6. An employee must have completed his probationary period to be eligible for vacaiton benefits. Benefits retroactive to date of hire.
7. No claim for sick leave or funeral leave shall be allowed which occurs during vacation.
8. Holidays are not charged to vacation time.
9. Nonprobationary employees who resign shall receive accrued vacation pay earned to the last complete month worked.
10. Employees dismissed shall receive accrued vacation pay earned through the last complete month worked.
11. Vacation time is not accumulative from one calendar year to the next.

ARTICLE X—SICK LEAVE

1. Full-time County employees shall earn one (1) day of paid sick leave for each month of employment with a maximum of sixty (60) days. Thereafter an employee with sixty (60) days of accumulated sick leave can earn one-half ($\frac{1}{2}$) day of sick leave for each month of employment for an additional sixty (60) days. The maximum accumulated sick leave shall be one hundred twenty (120) days.
   a. Regular part-time employees earn and accrue one-half ($\frac{1}{2}$) sick leave benefits.
2. Employees after serving a probationary period are eligible for sick leave benefits retroactive to the date of hire.
3. Accumulated sick leave credits are not paid when employment is terminated.
   a. Employees who retire at age sixty-five (65) shall be paid fifty (50) per cent of their accrued unused sick leave credits.
4. Recording the use of sick leave will be based on one-half ($\frac{1}{2}$) or one (1) day. Absence of less than one-quarter ($\frac{1}{4}$) day shall not be recorded or paid as sick leave; between one-quarter ($\frac{1}{4}$) and one-half ($\frac{1}{2}$) day, one half ($\frac{1}{2}$) will be recorded; between one-half ($\frac{1}{2}$) and one (1) day, one (1) will be recorded.
5. An employee may use up to three (3) days of accumulated paid sick leave for an absence necessitated by death of a parent, spouse,

child, brother, sister, mother-in-law, or father-in-law, when requested of the department head.

   a. In addition to the above, the employee may use up to three (3) days of accumulated sick leave for injury or illness of spouse or child while residing in the employee's home.

6. *Excluded Uses*

   a. Pregnancy is not considered an illness.

   b. Sick leave credits shall not accrue for absence in excess of thirty (30) calendar days.

   c. Injury incurred in supplemental employment.

7. *Substantiation*

   a. An employee shall substantiate the use of sick leave to his department head.

   b. No sick leave allowance will be made for the day before or after a holiday, or scheduled day/s/ off, without presenting a doctor's certificate of illness.

   c. Department heads shall require a medical certificate from a physician to justify the granting of sick leave in excess of two (2) days.

ARTICLE XI—HOSPITAL AND SURGICAL INSURANCE

Section I

The employer agrees to pay the full cost of a group hospital, surgical and major medical insurance plan for employees covered by this agreement and their dependents. The group plan shall be the same plan as available to all other County employees.

Section II

The employer agrees to pay one half (½) of life insurance premium not to exceed two dollars and twenty cents ($2.20) per month toward the cost of a group life insurance plan presently in effect.

ARTICLE XII—PENSION

In lieu of four (4) per cent increase in the employer's contribution to the Wisconsin Retirement Fund up to the first $7,800.00 in earnings, a salary increase of four (4) per cent on the first $7,800.00 in earnings. Effective January, 1971, this increase shall become part of the employer's contribution to the employee's share of the first $7,800.00 in contribution to the Wisconsin Retirement Fund.

ARTICLE XIII—JURY DUTY

1. Any employee subpoenaed for jury duty shall be paid the difference between his regular rate of pay and the pay received for jury duty.
2. Any employee subpoenaed as a witness connected with an incident occurring while on duty as an employee of the County shall be paid the difference between his regular rate of pay and the witness pay.

ARTICLE XIV—FUNERALS

1. Regular full-time employees shall be entitled to have one (1) day off with pay for the funeral of an immediate family including spouse, child, brother, sister, mother-in-law, father-in-law, sister-in-law, and parents.
   a. Regular part-time employees will be entitled to one-half (½) day's pay for the above reason.
2. Additional emergency leave may be taken with pay charged to accrued sick leave or compensatory time.

ARTICLE XV—MILEAGE REIMBURSEMENT

All employees required to use their own automobile in County business and approved by the department head shall be reimbursed at ten (10) cents per mile.

ARTICLE XVI—WORKMAN'S COMPENSATION

The County shall, without charge to sick leave, compensate an employee with full salary for three (3) calendar months per injury who is injured or becomes ill in the line of duty. The employee will assign his workman's compensation payments to the County.
   a. The above is contingent on the decision of the compensation carrier as to the duration of compensation.

ARTICLE XVII—TIME FOR NEGOTIATIONS

Section I

Agreement negotiations for 1971 shall be carried on by the parties as follows:
1. Submission of Union demands by August 1, 1970.

2. Submission of County's counterproposal or answer within three (3) weeks.
3. Conclusion of negotiations by October 1, 1970.

Section II

The adherence to the aforesaid schedule shall be effective as to its chronological order as closely as may be practical under the conditions applying at the time such conferences and negotiations are undertaken.

ARTICLE XVIII—IMPLEMENT OF THE AGREEMENT

Section I

Increases in compensation in the form of wages, payment of life insurance premium, and uniform allowance shall be retroactive to January 3, 1970, and shall apply to all employees of record at the date of execution of this agreement.

Section II

Overtime premium as provided in Article VI, Section II, shall apply at the beginning of the pay period following execution of this agreement.

Section III

Other articles of this agreement shall apply on the date of execution of this agreement.

ARTICLE XIX—TERMINATION

This agreement shall remain in full force and effect up to and including December 31, 1970, and shall continue in full force and effect thereafter until such time that either party desires to open, amend, or otherwise change this agreement.
Dated this 1st day of July, 1970.

THE COUNTY OF WAUKESHA BY:
E. Vernon Metcalf, Chairman
Negotiating Committee

Lloyd G. Owens
County Board Chairman
Richard Sylvester
County Clerk

TEAMSTERS UNION LOCAL NO. 695 BY:
A. E. Mueller, Consultant

Glen Van Kuren
Assistant Secretary/Treasurer

Kenneth Ludwigsen, Chairman
Negotiating Committee

John Willert
Association President

Appendix D

September 17, 1970

TO: Area Director, General Organizers, Joint Councils,
and Local Unions

Attached is a survey of Teamster organization of public employees —state, county, municipal and other public authorities—prepared by the Research Department of the International Union. The attached survey indicates that Teamster local unions represent about 60,000 public employees—at all levels of public employment.

I strongly urge you to review this study, and to use it as a springboard to develop an organizing campaign among public employees at all levels of government.

This is a fertile field for expanding Teamster membership. Unionization of public employees has been described as the "growth stock" of American trade unions. Unionization of public employees has been facilitated by recent legislation recognizing the right of public employees to organize and to negotiate collective bargaining agreements. For example, the Pennsylvania Legislature passed a bill, effective October 21, 1970, known as the Public Employees Bill which gives public employees employed by the state, county, and municipalities the right to organize.

The Teamsters Union is no Johnny-come-lately to the field of public employee unionism. We have represented such employees and bargained for them for decades.

In 1968, the International City Managers' Association surveyed the extent of union representation in cities with 10,000 or more population. The survey states: "Outside the State, County, and Municipal Employees, the Teamsters Union seems to have had the greatest success in organizing municipal employees in a variety of functions."

The survey concludes: "The across-the-board nature of Teamster representation also shows up in the fact that it represents employees in independent as well as in central and suburban areas and it cities with various forms of government. It is clear—that the Teamsters is a union to be reckoned with in municipal employee-management relations."

161

Our own survey shows that 170 Teamster locals (about one out of every five) represent and bargain for public employees. We have just begun to scratch the surface. The time is ripe; legislation is favorable; the Teamsters have long and favorable experience in organizing city, state, and county employees; their contracts rank among the best in the field of public employment.

The General Executive Board has gone on record favoring expansion of our organizing efforts among public employees. This is a challenge which we can and should meet successfully. Public employees *can* be organized, and by the Teamsters Union. This study by our Research Department is a useful tool for organization.

The Research Department has assembled a comprehensive file of Teamster contracts covering all types of public employees. Copies of such contracts, which can be used for organizing and bargaining, may be obtained by writing to the International Union Research Department, 25 Louisiana Avenue, N.W., Washington, D.C. 20001.

Best wishes.

Fraternally yours,
Frank E. Fitzsimmons
General Vice President

FEF:lgj
Enclosure

TEAMSTER
UNION REPRESENTATION AND BARGAINING AMONG PUBLIC EMPLOYEES
Spring 1970

A total of 170 Teamster local unions are authorized bargaining agents for more than 57,000 employees who work for city, county, state, and Federal governments and other public authorities. Recognition is granted by written agreements, local ordinances and oral recognition.

Level of Government

Slightly over 60 percent of Teamster-represented public employees work for a city or municipality, and an additional nine percent for a municipal special authority, such as Municipal Housing Authorities.

About one-half of all Teamster-represented municipal employees are located in New York City (19,043 employees).

In all, therefore, 7 out of every 10 public employees working under Teamster-negotiated contracts or represented by Teamster local unions operate at the city, town, or village level.

County employees account for slightly under 10 percent and state employees comprise six percent of the 57,000 public employees for whom the Teamsters bargain. (See Table 1).

TABLE 1

TEAMSTER ORGANIZATION OF PUBLIC EMPLOYEES
BY LEVEL OF GOVERNMENT

Level of Government	No. Employees	% of Total
Federal	339	0.1
State	3,529	6.2
County	5,187	9.1
Municipal	35,462	62.1
School District	3,972	7.0
Public College or University	2,387	4.2
Special Authority—Federal	22	*
Special Authority—State	897	1.6
Special Authority—County	47	*
Special Authority—Municipal	5,281	9.2
Total	57,123	100.0[1]

*Less than 1%.
[1]Total does not equal 100% due to rounding.

163

Type of Function or Activity

As shown in Table 2, 27.8% of the public employees represented by the Teamsters are engaged in providing sanitary services, such as sewage and refuse collection.

Local 831 in New York City represents 10,000 of the total of about 16,000 Teamster-organized public employees engaged in such activities.

Street and Highway Department employees ranked second—accounting for about 25% of the total; non-instructional personnel in Public Education ranked third, accounting for slightly over 12 percent; and Public Welfare employees (Public Housing & Social Services), ranked fourth, accounting for 10 percent. (See Table 2).

Other functions represented by Teamster unions include Parks & Recreation, Police and Fire Protection, Public Utilities, Public Health and Hospitals, Public Transportation, and other public activities.

Geographic Representation

The Northeast and Middle Atlantic States account for more than half (30,229 out of 57,123), of the Teamster-organized public employees. New York State alone accounts for 21,400 of these employees.

About 20,000 government employees are located in the mid-West, with over 11,500 in the states of Illinois and Michigan. The mid-Western states together account for about 35% of the total.

Slightly over 5,000 (or 9.1%) of the Teamster-organized public employees are located in the Far West. California accounts for about one-third of this group.

TABLE 2

TEAMSTER ORGANIZATION OF PUBLIC EMPLOYEES
BY FUNCTION OR ACTIVITY

Type of Function or Activity	No. Employees	% of Total
Police Protection	2,349	4.1
Fire Protection	1,312	2.3
Street and Highway	14,116	24.7
Parks and Recreation	3,448	6.0
Sanitary Service	15,883	27.8
Public Utilities	2,260	4.0
Public Health and Hospitals	1,928	3.4
Public Education (non-instructional)	7,014	12.3
Public Welfare	5,762	10.1
Public Transportation	1,231	2.2
Other Functions	1,820	3.2
Total	57,123	100.0

A total of 1,500 government employees represented by the Teamsters are located in the Southern states, primarily in New Orleans, Louisiana. (See Table 3).

Prepared by
Research Department
International Brotherhood
of Teamsters
September, 1970

TABLE 3

TEAMSTER ORGANIZATION OF PUBLIC EMPLOYEES
BY STATE AND AREA CONFERENCE

Central Conference

Illinois	6,809	Missouri	405
Indiana	2,182	Nebraska	——
Iowa	382	North Dakota	137
Kansas	92	Ohio	2,017
Kentucky	410	South Dakota	——
Michigan	4,717	Wisconsin	1,512
Minnesota	1,513	Total	20,176

Eastern Conference

Connecticut	676	Pennsylvania	4,009
Delaware	80	Rhode Island	20
Maine	——	South Carolina	——
Maryland	12	Vermont	——
Massachusetts	1,294	Virginia	——
New Hampshire	——	West Virginia	——
New Jersey	2,738	Washington, D. C.	——
New York	21,400	Total	30,229
North Carolina	——		

Southern Conference

Alabama	215	Mississippi	——
Arkansas	——	Oklahoma	——
Florida	——	Tennessee	88
Georgia	——	Texas	——
Louisiana	1,195	Total	1,498

Western Conference

Alaska	44	Nevada	——
Arizona	66	New Mexico	8
California	1,633	Oregon	65
Colorado	170	Utah	——
Hawaii	——	Washington	2,479
Idaho	72	Wyoming	——
Montana	683	Total	5,220

Total All Conferences: 57,123

PUBLIC EMPLOYEE ORGANIZATIONS
(Government Code)

(Meyers - Milias - Brown Act as amended 1968)

Effective January 1, 1969

3500. *Purpose of chapter.*

It is the purpose of this chapter to promote full communication between public employers and their employees by providing a reasonable method of resolving disputes regarding wages, hours, and other terms and conditions of employment between public employers and public employee organizations. It is also the purpose of this chapter to promote the improvement of personnel management and employer-employee relations within the various public agencies in the State of California by providing a uniform basis for recognizing the right of public employees to join organizations of their own choice and be represented by such organizations in their employment relationships with public agencies. Nothing contained herein shall be deemed to supersede the provisions of existing state law and the charters, ordinances and rules of local public agencies which establish and regulate a merit or civil service system or which provide for other methods of administering employer-employee relations. This chapter is intended, instead, to strengthen merit, civil service and other methods of administering employer-employee relations through the establishment of uniform and orderly methods of communication between employees and the public agencies by which they are employed. (Amended 1968).

3501. *"Employee organization": "Recognized employee organization" "Public agency": "Public employee": "Mediation."*

As used in this chapter:

(a) "Employee organization" means any organization which includes employees of a public agency and which has as one of its primary purpose representing such employees in their relations with that public agency.

(b) "Recognized employee organization" means an employee organization which has been formally acknowledged by the public agency as an employee organization that represents employees of the public agency.

(c) Except as otherwise provided in this subdivision, "public agency" means the State of California, every governmental subdivision, every district, every public and quasi-public corporation, every public agency and public service corporation and every town, city, county, city and county and municipal corporation, whether incorporated or not and whether chartered or not. As used in this chapter, "public agency" does not mean a school district or a county board of education or a county superintendent of schools or a personnel commission in a school district having a merit system as provided in Chapter 3 (commencing with Section 13580) of Division 10 of the Education Code.

(d) "Public employee" means any person employed by any public agency excepting those persons elected by popular vote or appointed to office by the Governor of this State.

(e) "Mediation" means effort by an impartial third party to assist in reconciling a dispute regarding wages, hours and other terms and conditions of employment between representatives of the public agency and the recognized employee organization or recognized employee organizations through interpretation, suggestion and advice. (Amended 1968).

3502. *Right of public employees to choose and partake in activities of employee organizations for representation in employer-employee relations: Rights of refusal to join and of self-representation.*

Except as otherwise provided by the Legislature, public employees shall have the right to form, join, and participate in the activities of employee organizations of their own choosing for the purpose of representation on all matters of employer-employee relations. Public employees also shall have the right to refuse to join or participate in the activities of employee organizations and shall have the right to represent themselves individually in their employment relations with the public agency.

3503. *Employee organizations: Representation of members in employment relations: Membership regulations: Self-representation.*

Recognized employee organizations shall have the right to represent their members in their employment relations with public agencies. Employee organizations may establish reasonable restrictions regarding who may join and may make reasonable provisions for the dismissal of individuals from membership. Nothing in this section shall prohibit any employee from appearing in his own behalf in his employment relations with the public agency. (Amend 1968).

3504. *Scope of representation.*

The scope of representation shall include all matters relating to employment conditions and employer-employee relations, including, but not limited to, wages, hours, and other terms and conditions of employment, except, however, that the scope of representation shall not include consideration of the merits, necessity, or organization of any service or activity provided by law or executive order. (Amended 1968).

3504.5

Except in cases of emergency as provided in this section, the governing body of a public agency, and boards and commissions designated by law or by such governing body, shall give reasonable written notice to each recognized employee organization affected of any ordinance, rule, resolution or regulation directly relating to matters within the scope of representation proposed to be adopted by the governing body or such boards and commissions and shall give such recognized employee organization the opportunity to meet with the governing body or such boards and commissions.

In cases of emergency when the governing body or such boards and commissions determine that an ordinance, rule, resolution or regulation must be adopted immediately without prior notice or meeting with a recognized employee organization, the governing body or such boards and commissions shall provide such notice and opportunity to meet at the earliest practicable time following the adoption of such ordinance, rule, resolution, or regulation. (Amended 1968).

3505. *Meetings of representatives of public agency and employee organizations. Consideration of presentations by employee organization.*

The governing body of a public agency, or such boards, commissions, administrative officers or other representatives as may be properly designated by law or by such governing body, shall meet and confer in good faith regarding wages, hours, and other terms and conditions of employment with representatives of recognized employee organizations, as defined in subdivision (b) of Section 3501, and shall consider fully such presentations as are made by the employee organization on behalf of its members prior to arriving at a determination of policy or course of action.

"Meet and confer in good faith" means that a public agency, or such representatives as it may designate, and representatives of recognized employee organizations, shall have the mutual obligation personally to meet and confer in order to exchange freely information, opinions, and propsals, and to endeavor to reach agreement on matters within the scope of representation. (Amended 1968).

3505.1

If agreement is reached by the representatives of the public agency and a recognized employee organization or recognized employee organizations, they shall jointly prepare a written memorandum of such understanding, which shall not be binding, and present it to the governing body or its statutory representative for determination. (Amended 1968).

3505.2

If after a reasonable period of time, representatives of the public agency and the recognized employee organization fail to reach agreement, the public agency and the recognized employee or recognized employee organizations together may agree upon the appointment of a mediator mutually agreeable to the parties. Costs of mediation shall be divided one-half to the public agency and one-half to the recognized employee organization or recognized employee organizations. (Amended 1968).

3505.3

Public agencies shall allow a reasonable number of public agency employee representatives of recognized employee organizations reasonable time off without loss of compensation or other benefits when formally meeting and conferring with representatives of the public agency on matters within the scope of representation. (Amended 1968).

3506. *Public agencies and employee organizations not to act to detriment of employee because of exercise of rights under Sec. 3502.*

Public agencies and employee organizations shall not interfere with, intimidate, restrain, coerce or discriminate against public employees because of their exercise of their rights under Section 3502.

3507. *Rules and regulations: Permissible provisions: State Personnel Board.*

A public agency may adopt reasonable rules and regulations after consultation in good faith with representatives of an employee organization or organizations for the administration of employer-employee relations under this chapter (commencing with Section 3500).

Such rules and regulations may include provisions for (a) verifying that an organization does in fact represent employees of the public agency (b) verifying the official status of employee organization officers and representatives (c) recognition of employee organizations (d) additional procedures for the resolution of disputes involving wages, hours and other terms and conditions of employment (e) access of employee organization officers and representatives to work locations (f) use of official bulletin boards and other means of communication by employee organizations (g) furnishing nonconfidential information pertaining to employment relations to employee organizations (h) such other matters as are necessary to carry out the purposes of this chapter. For employees in the state civil service rules and regulations in accordance with this section may be adopted by the State Personnel Board. (Amended 1968).

3507.3

Professional employees shall not be denied the right to be represented separately from nonprofessional employees by a professional employee organization consisting of such professional employees.

"Professional employees," for the purpose of this section, means employees engaged in work requiring specialized knowledge and skills attained through completion of a recognized course of instruction, including, but not limited to, attorneys, physcans, registered nurses, engineers, architects, teachers, and various types of physical, chemical, and biological scientists. (Amended 1968).

3507.5

In addition to those rules and regulations a public agency may adopt pursuant to and in the same manner as in Section 3507, any such agency may adopt reasonable rules and regulations providing for designation of the management and confidential employees of the public agency and restricting such employees from representing any employee organization, which represents other employees of the public agency, on matters within the scope of representation. (Amended 1968).

3508. *Power of public agency to limit or prohibit employee participation in employee organizations: Positions concerning law enforcement: No other ground: Exception.*

The governing body of a public agency may, in accordance with reasonable standards, designate positions or classes of positions which have duties consisting primarily of the enforcement of state laws or local ordinances, and may by resolution or ordinance adopted after a public hearing, limit or prohibit the right of employees in such positions or classes of positions to form, join or participate in employee organizations where it is in the public interest to do so, however the governing body may not prohibit the right of its employees who are full-time "peace officers," as that term is defined in Section 817 of the Penal Code, to join or participate in employee organizations which are composed solely of such peace officers, which concern themselves solely and exclusively with the wages, hours, working conditions, welfare programs, and advancement of the academic and vocational training in furtherance of the police profession, and which are not subordinance to any other organization.

The right of employees to form, join and participate in the activities of employee organizations shall not be restricted by a public agency on any grounds other than those set forth in this section. (Amended 1968).

3509. *Lab C. Sec. 923 not applicable to public employees.*

The enactment of this chapter shall not be construed as making the provisions of Section 923 of the Labor Code applicable to public employees.

SENATE BILL NO. 333

Introduced by Senator Dills

February 18, 1971

REFERRED TO COMMITTEE ON INDUSTRIAL RELATIONS

An act to amend Section 3501 of, and to add Chapter 10.5 (commencing with Section 3525) to Division 4 of Title 1 of, the Government Code, and to repeal Chapter 4 (commencing with Section 1960) of Part 6 of Division 2 of the Labor Code, relating to public employees.

LEGISLATIVE COUNSEL'S DIGEST

SB 333, as introduced, Dills (I.R.). Local safety employees.

Amends Sec. 3501, adds Ch. 10.5 (commencing with Sec. 3525), Div. 4, Title 1, Gov. C., repeals Ch. 4 (commencing with Sec. 1960), Pt. 6, Div. 2, Lab. C.

Requires that, upon request, public agencies meet and confer with recognized employee organizations representing a majority of the local safety employees and requires parties to attempt to reach agreement on matters under consideration. Specifies that such employees do not have the right to strike or to recognize a picket line of a labor organization while in the course of the performance of their official duties.

Defines "local safety employee," "recognition," and "to meet and confer."

Specifies that failure to give certain information and notices shall invalidate any action of a governing body.

Provides procedure to be followed when parties reach agreement or fail to reach agreement, including provisions for binding findings and recommendations by a board of review in the event agreement cannot be reached.

Requires public agencies to allow officers and representatives of employee organizations of local safety employees reasonable time off without loss of any benefits to prepare for representation and to represent employees of the public agencies within the scope of the employee organizations' representation of local safety employees of public agencies.

Provides that enactment of provisions shall not be construed to alter any right granted to, or withheld from, public employees, other than local safety employees, under any constitutional or statutory law or judicial decision.

Vote—Majority; Appropriation—No; Fiscal Committee—No.

The people of the State of California do enact as follows:
SECTION 1. Section 3501 of the Government Code is amended to read:

3501. As used in this chapter:

(a) "Employee organization" means any organization which includes employees of a public agency and which has as one of its primary purposes representing such employees in their relations with that public agency.

(b) "Recognized employee organization" means an employee organization which has been formally acknowledged by the public agency as an employee organization that represents employees of the public agency.

(c) Except as otherwise provided in this subdivision, "public agency" means the State of California, every governmental subdivision, every district, every public and quasi-public corporation, every public agency and public service corporation and every town, city, county, city and county and municipal corporation, whether incorporated or not and whether chartered or not. As used in this chapter, "public agency" does not mean a school district or a county board of education or a county superintendent of schools or a personnel commission in a school district having a merit system as provided in Chapter 3 (commencing with Section 13580) of Division 10 of the Education Code.

(d) "Public employee" means any person employed by any public agency, including employees of the fire departments and fire services of the state, excepting those persons *subject to the provisions of Chapter 10.5 (commencing with Section 3525) of this division and persons* elected by popular vote or appointed to office by the Governor of this state.

(e) "Mediation" means effort by an impartial third party to assist in reconciling a dispute regarding wages, hours and other terms and conditions of employment between representatives of the public agency and the recognized employee organization or recognized employee organizations through interpretation, suggestion and advice.

SEC. 2. Chapter 10.5 (commencing with Section 3525) is added to Division 4 of Title 1 of the Government Code, to read:

CHAPTER 10.5. LOCAL SAFETY
EMPLOYEE ORGANIZATIONS

3525. It is the purpose of this chapter to promote the improvement of personnel management and employer-employee relations with respect to local safety employees within the various public agencies in the State of California by providing a uniform basis for recognizing the right of local safety employees to join organizations of their own choice and be represented by such organizations in their employment relationships with public agencies. Nothing contained herein shall be deemed to supersede the provisions of existing state law and the charters, ordinances and rules of local public agencies which establish and regulate a merit or civil service system. This chapter in intended, instead, to strengthen merit or civil service systems administering such employer-employee relations through the establishment of uniform and orderly methods of communication between local safety employees and the public agencies by which they are employed.

3526. As used in this chapter:

(a) "Employee organization" means any organization which includes local safety employees of a public agency and which has as one of its primary purposes representing such employees in their relations with that public agency.

(b) "Public agency" means every public entity which employs local safety employees.

(c) "Local safety employee" means any city policeman, constable, sheriff, deputy sheriff, marshal, deputy marshal, district attorney investigator, city fireman, county fireman, or fireman of any fire district of the state.

(d) As used in Section 3530 "recognition" means the act of a public agency formally recognizing the employee organizations which represent a majority of local safety employees of the public agency. A public agency shall recognize an employee organization which represents a majority of the employees of the entity. No public agency shall unreasonably withhold recognition of employee organizations.

3527. Except as otherwise provided by the Legislature, local safety employees shall have the right to form, join, and participate in the activities of employee organizations of their own choosing for the purpose of representation on all matters of employer-employee relations. Local safety employees also shall have the right to refuse to join or participate in the activities of employee organizations and shall have the right to represent themselves individually in their employment relations with the public agency.

3528. Employee organizations shall have the right to represent their members in their employment relations with public agencies. Employee organizations may establish reasonable restrictions regarding who may join and may make reasonable provisions for the dismissal of individuals from membership. Nothing in this section shall prohibit any employee from appearing in his own behalf in his employment relations with the public agency.

3529. The scope of representation shall include all matters relating to employment conditions and employer-employee relations, including, but not limited to, wages, hours, and other terms and conditions of employment.

3530. Upon request, the governing body of a public agency, or such boards, commissions, administrative officers or other representatives as may be properly designated by law or by such governing body, shall meet and confer, as defined in Section 3505, with representatives of recognized employee organizations representing a majority of the local safety employees, and such representatives of the public agency and the representatives of the employee organizaiton shall attempt to reach agreement on matters under consideration. Local safety employees shall not have the right to strike, or to recognize a picket line of a labor organization while in the course of the performance of their official duties. As used in this section "strike" includes any strike or other concerted stoppage of work by local safety employees, and any concerted slowdown or other concerted interruption of operations by such employees.

3530.1. To meet and confer shall include the right of each representative of a recognized employee organization:

(a) To be informed on all matters within the scope of representation,

(b) To be given reasonable notice of any action proposed to be taken by a public agency, board, or commission, which action relates to matters within the scope of representation.

Failure to comply with the provisions of (a) and (b) above shall invalidate any action of the governing body.

3531. When the parties reach agreement under Section 3530 and the agreement is not subject to action by the governing body, they shall prepare a written memorandum of such agreement.

When the parties reach agreement under Section 3530 and the agreement is subject to action by the governing body, they shall prepare a written memorandum of such agreement and submit it to the governing body.

If after a reasonable time the parties do not reach agreement, each party shall, within 10 days, and no less than 60 days prior to the date set by law for the fixing of the tax rate for the coming fiscal year, submit to the other party, and to the governing body in those cases where any agreement is subject to action by the governing body, a statement of its position and reasons therefor.

3532. If after a reasonable period of time, agreement cannot be reached under Section 3530, either party may submit this disagreement to a three-member board of review. After such referral, the board of review shall acquire such facts, take such testimony, and interview such witnesses as it deems necessary, and shall, not less than 10 days prior to the time set by law for the fixing of the tax rate, or such greater or lesser time period to what the parties shall mutually agree, present its findings and recommendations in written form to the parties. The findings and recommendations of the board of review shall be conclusive and binding upon the parties. The expenses of the board of review shall be shared equally by the parties unless the board determines one party has not met and conferred in good faith, in which event such party shall pay all expenses of the board of review. including expert witness and attorney fees.

3533. The three-member board of review required in accordance with the provisions of Section 3532 shall be selected as follows: The board, commission, administrative officers, or other representatives with whom the employee organization is negotiating shall, within three days after the date on which the establishment of a board of review has been demanded, select one member of such board; the employee organization concerned shall within three days thereafter, select one member; and the two members thus chosen shall, within three days thereafter, select a third impartial member, but in the event that these two members are unable to agree on the selection of the impartial mmber, then such members shall be selected within the three-day period set forth above, from a list of nine persons skilled in employer-employee relations matters which list shall be composed as follows; the two members shall request three names from each of the following organizations namely, the American Arbitration Association, the Federal Mediation and Conciliation Service, and the State Conciliation Service of the State of California. On receipt of such list, the employer member shall first strike one name and the parties shall thereafter each alternately strike one name from such list, until only one name remains thereon. The person whose name remains shall be the third impartial member of the board of review.

3534. In making its findings and recommendations the board of review shall consider the prevailing wage in comparable public and private employment, safety of the public, consumer price index and changes therein, workload, and the nature of the risk involved in the hours and type of work.

3535. Public agencies and employee organizations shall not interfere with, intimidate, restrain, coerce or discriminate against public employees because of their exercise of their rights under Section 3527.

3536. Public agencies shall allow officers and representatives of employee organizations of local safety employees reasonable time off without loss of compensation or any other employee benefits in order to prepare for representation and to represent employes of the public agencies within the scope of the employee organizations' representation of th local safety employees of the public agencies.

3537. A public agency may adopt reasonable rules and regulations for the administration of employer-employee relations under this chapter.

Such rules and regulations may include provisions for (a) verifying that an organization does in fact represent local safety employees of the public agency (b) verifying the official status of employee organization officers and representatives (c) access of employee organization officers and representatives to work locations (d) use of official bulletin boards and other means of communication by employee organizations (e) furnishing nonconfidential information pertaining to employment relations to employee organizations (f) such other matters as are necessary to carry out the purposes of this chapter.

3538. The governing body of a public agency may, in accordance with reasonable standards, by resolution or ordinance adopted after a public hearing, limit or prohibit the right of local safety employees to form, join or participate in employee organizations where it is in the public interest to do so; however, the governing body may not prohibit the right of its local safety employees who are full-time "peace officers," as that term is defined in Section 830.1 to 830.3, inclusive, of the Penal Code, to join or participate in employee organizations which are composed solely of such peace officers, which concern themselves solely and exclusively with the wages, hours, working conditions, welfare programs, and advancement of the acadamic and vocational training in furtherance of the police profession, and which are not subordinate to any other organization.

The right of employees to form, join and participate in the activities of employee organizations shall not be restricted by a public agency on any grounds other than those set forth in this section.

3539. The enactment of this chapter shall not be construed as making the provisions of Section 923 of the Labor Code applicable to local law enforcement employees. The enactment of this chapter shall not be construed to alter any right granted to, or withheld from, public employees, other than local safety employees, under any constitutional or statutory law or judicial decision.

SEC. 3. Chapter 4 (commencing with Section 1960) of part 6 of Division 2 of the Labor Code is repealed.

BIBLIOGRAPHY

BOOKS

Bok., Derek C. and John T. Dunlop: *Labor and the American Community.* New York, Simon and Schuster, 1970.

Brissenden, P. F.: *The I.W.W.* New York, Columbia University Press, 1920.

Brooks, R. R. R.: *When Labor Organizes.* New Haven, Yale University Press, 1937.

Burpo, John H.: *The Police Labor Movement.* Springfield, Charles C Thomas Publisher, 1971.

Commons, John R. and associates (Eds.): *A Documentary History of American Industrial Society.* Cleveland, Arthur H. Clark, 1910.

Commons, John R. and associates: *History of Labour in the United States.* New York, Macmillan, 1918.

Dacus, J. A.: *Annals of the Great Strikes.* St. Louis, Scammel, 1877.

Dulles, Foster R.: *Labor in America.* New York, Thomas Y. Crowell, 1966.

Fosdick, Raymond B.: *American Police Systems.* New York, The Century Company, 1921.

French, Wendell: *The Personnel Management Process: Human Resources Administration.* Boston, Houghton Mifflin, 1964.

Gompers, Samuel: *Seventy Years of Life and Labor.* New York, E. P. Dutton, 1945.

Lavine, Emanuel H.: *Cheese It—The Cops.* New York, Vanguard Press, 1936.

Lorwin, L. L.: *The American Federation of Labor.* Washington, D.C., The Brookings Institute, 1933.

Martin, Edward W.: *The History of the Great Riots.* Philadelphia, National Publishing, 1877.

Powderly, Terence V.: *Thirty Years of Labor.* Philadelphia, T. V. Powderly, 1890.

Reynolds, Lloyd G.: *Labor Economics and Labor Relations.* New York, Prentice-Hall, 1954.

Schweppe, Emma: *The Firemen's and Patrolmen's Unions in the City of New York.* New York, King's Crown Press, 1948.

Skolnick, Jerome: *Justice Without Trial.* New York, John Wiley & Sons, 1966.

Smith, Bruce: *Police Systems in the United States.* New York, Harper and Brothers, 1940.

Spero, Sterling D.: *Government as Employer.* New York, Remsen Press, 1948.
Stewart, Frank M.: *The National Civil Service League.* Austin, University of Texas, 1929.
Taft, Philip: *Organized Labor in American History.* New York, Harper & Row, 1964.
Walsh, J. R.: *CIO: Industrial Unionism in Action.* New York, W. W. Norton, 1937.
Ware, Norman J.: *The Labor Movement in the United States, 1860-1895.* New York, D. Appleton, 1929.
Webb, Sidney and Beatrice: *Industrial Democracy.* London, Longmans, Green, 1914.
Williamson, T. S. and Herbert Harris: *Trends in Collective Bargaining.* New York, Twentieth Century Fund, 1945.
Zeisler, Ernest B.: *The Haymarket Riot.* Chicago, Alexander J. Isaacs, 1958.
Ziskind, David: *One Thousand Strikes of Government Employees.* New York, Columbia University Press, 1940.

PERIODICALS

Andrews, Louis C.: What's the law—police labor unions. *Michigan Municipal Review, 34*(12):318, December 1961.
Baldwin, Roger L.: Have public employees the right to strike? yes. *National Municipal Review, 30*:515-517, September 1941.
Berrodin, Eugene F.: At the bargaining table. *National Civic Review, 56*(7):392-398, July 1967.
Berrodin, Eugene F.: Cross-currents in public employee bargaining. *Public Personnel Review, 29*(4):217-221, October 1968.
Blum, David E.: The law and public employee unions. *American County Government,* December 1966. p. 12.
Burda, D. J. and A. J. Reiss, Jr.: Command, control, and charisma: reflections on police bureaucracy. *American Journal of Sociology,* July 1966, pp. 68-76.
Cohen, Frederick: Legal aspects of unionization among public employees. *Temple Law Quarterly,* Winter 1957, pp. 187-199.
Cornell, Herbert: Collective bargaining by public employee groups. *University of Pennsylvania Law Review,* November 1958, pp. 44-65.
Davies, Audrey M.: History and legality of police unions. *GRA Reporter, 5*:42, July-August 1953.
Foulke, William Dudley: Labor unions in the civil service. *Good Government, 35*:120, 1918.
Fox, V.: Sociological and political aspects of police administration. *Sociology and Sociological Research, 51*(1):39-48, October 1966.

Goldstein, Herman: Administrative problems in controlling the exercise of police authority. *Journal of Criminal Law, Criminology, and Police Science, 58* (2):160-172, June 1967.

Hepbron, James M.: Police unionization means disorganization. *American City,* November 1958, pp. 131-132.

Heustis, Carl E.: Police unions, *Journal of Criminal Law, Criminology, and Police Science, 48*:644, November 1958.

Holladay, Roy E.: Police unions—programs of negation. *Police,* November-December 1961, pp. 63-66.

Kaplan, H. Eliot: Have public employees the right to strike? No. *National Municipal Review, 30*:518, September 1941.

Kennedy, Stephen P.: No union for New York City police. *American City,* October 1958, p. 179.

Keresman, Peter: Constructive employee relations in police departments. *Labor Law Journal,* August 1957, pp. 556-558.

Klaus, Ida: Labor relations in the public service: exploration and experiment. *Syracuse Law Journal,* Spring 1959, pp. 182-202.

Lipset, Seymour M.: Why police hate liberals and vice-versa. *Atlantic Monthly,* March 1969, p. 79.

Lowenberg, Joseph: Labor relations for policemen and firefighters. *Monthly Labor Review, 91*:36, May 1968.

McKelvey, Jean T.: The role of state agencies in public employee labor relations. *Industrial Labor Relations Review, 20*(2):179-197, January 1967.

Mire, Joseph: Collective bargaining in the public service. *American Economic Review, 36*:347-358, 1946.

Murray, Edmund P.: Should Police Unionize, *The Nation,* June 13, 1959, p. 533.

Mysliwiec, Frank A.: Municipal employees' unions: the climb-up the ladder. *Duquesne University Law Review, (4):137-146,* Fall 1965.

Nichols, Marion C.: The boston police system. *The Christian Register,* October 1919.

Padway, Joseph A.: Collective bargaining in government enterprise. *Lawyers Guild Review, (2):1-7,* March 1942.

Ramage, Richard J.: Labor relations—labor relations acts—public employment—right of police officers to unionize. *North Dakota Law Review,* July 1959, pp. 236-238.

Raskin, A. H.: Strikes by public employees. *Atlantic,* January 1968, pp. 46-51.

Sackley, Arthur M.: Trends in police and fire salaries. *Monthly Labor Review, 88:160-161,* February 1965.

Spero, Sterling D.: Collective bargaining in public employment: form and scope. *Public Administration Review, 22:1-5,* 1962.

Spero, Sterling D.: Have public employees the right to strike? maybe. *National Municipal Review, 30-524,* September 1941.

Stone, Donald C.: Police and Strikes. *The Survey, 71:102,* April 1935.

Tead, Ordway: Labor unions in a democratic state. *Good Government, 35:133-135,* 1918.

Weisenfeld, Allan: Public employees—first or second class citizens. *Labor Law Journal,* November 1965, pp. 685-704.

Wurf, Jerry: Coming unionized government. *Public Employee,* October 1966, p. 6.

AFL-CIO police union. *Newsweek,* March 3, 1969, p. 73.

Baltimore police union chartered. *Public Employee,* April 1966, p. 4.

Blue power. *Wall Street Journal,* October 20, 1967, p. 16.

Collective negotiations in the public service: A symposium. *Public Administration Review,* March-April 1968, p. 111-147.

Connecticut police local gains a $920 increase. *Public employee,* March 1967, p. 10.

Local associations of municipal employees. *Urban Data Service,* International City Management Association, *2:1,* January 1970.

Now policemen are joining the teamsters. *U. S. News and World Report,* January 16, 1967, p. 8.

Omaha police get 15% pay increases. *Public Employee,* November 1966, p. 5.

Police union authorized. *AFL-CIO News,* February 22, 1969, p. 1.

Right of municipal employees' union to strike and to bargain collectively. *Minnesota Law Review, 34:260-266,* 1950.

SCME vs. North Platte, Nebraska. *AFL-CIO News,* January 4, 1969, p. 3.

Unions enter city hall. *Public Management,* September 1966, pp. 244-252.

When police walked out in New York. *U. S. News and World Report,* February 1, 1971, p. 42.

When policemen strike in a big city: Detroit. *U. S. News and World Report,* July 3, 1967, pp. 73-74.

Wisconsin court permits police union. *Public Employee,* November 1966, p. 10.

PAMPHLETS

Collective Bargaining for State and Local Public Employees, Champaign-Urbana, Institute of Labor and Industrial Relations, University of Illinois, 1966.

Hanslowe, Kurt: *The Emerging Law of Labor Relations in Public Employment.* Institute of Labor and Industrial Relations Paperback No. 4, Ithaca, New York, Cayuga Press, 1967.

Kirwan, William E.: *The New York State Police: History and Development of Collective Negotiations,* Albany, New York, Superintendent, New York State Police, 1969.

Miller, Glenn W.: *Collective Bargaining by Public Employees,* Columbus, Labor Education and Research Service, 1966.

Padway, Joseph A.: Policemen have a constitutional right to form and join labor unions. *Bulletin of American Federation of State, County and Municipal Employees,* 1944.

Rhyme, Charles S.: *Labor Unions and Municipal Employees Law,* Washington, D. C., National Institute of Municipal Law Officers, 1946.

Rubin, Richard S.: A summary of state collective bargaining law in public employment. *Public Employee Relations Report No. 3,* Cornell University, Ithaca, New York, 1967.

Stewart, Ethelbert: A documentary history of early organization of printers. *Bulletin of the Department of Labor,* November 1905.

Thompson, Andrew W. J.: Unit determination in public employment. *Public Employee Relations Report No. 1,* Cornell University, Ithaca, New York, 1967.

Thompson, Andrew W. J.: Strikes and strike penalties in public employment. *Public Employee Relations Report No. 2,* Cornell University, Ithaca, New York, 1967.

Police Unions, Bulletin on Police Problems, rev. ed., Washington, D.C., International Association of Chiefs of Police, August 1958.

Police Unions and Other Police Organizations, Bulletin No. 4, Washington, D. C., International Association of Chiefs of Police, 1944.

NEWSPAPERS

Fox, Sylvan: Why policemen are unhappy. *New York Times,* October 24, 1968, p. 59.

Raskin, A. H.: Hoffa regrets police union attempt. *New York Times,* January 1, 1959, p. 1.

A labor milestone for police. *The Sacramento Union,* August 23, 1967.

Absent police return to duty in Springfield. *Sacramento Bee,* January 16, 1971.

AFL-CIO charters a police union. *San Francisco Chronicle,* February 21, 1969, p. 2.

Another executive council meeting on strike tonight, *Vallejo News Chronicle,* July 18, 1969, p. 1.

Antioch police ask aid in wage talks. *Antioch Daily Ledger,* July 2, 1970, p. 1.

Antioch police vote to strike Saturday; tax election planned. *Antioch Daily Ledger,* July 9, 1970, p. 1.

Cassese calls contract unacceptable. *New York Times,* December 5, 1968, p. 1.

City braces for police strike. *Antioch Daily Ledger,* July 10, 1970, p. 1.

Bill calls for settlement of firemen, police strikes by compulsory arbitration. *Sacramento Bee,* February 18, 1971.

Chief patrols in Hollister police strike. *San Francisco Examiner,* November 13, 1970.

City council has made fair offer. *Vallejo News Chronicle,* July 21, 1969, p. 1.

City police reject final 8.5% hike. *Antioch Daily Ledger,* July 3, 1970, p. 1.

City police strike settled. *Antioch Daily Ledger,* July 14, 1970, p. 1.

City wants to talk. *Antioch Daily Ledger,* July 2, 1970, p. 1.

Detroit policemen get raise. *New York Times,* February 28, 1967, p. 37.

Embattled police taking the offensive. *The Washington Post Outlook,* December 15, 1968, p. B1, B5.

Extra effort helps avert city crisis. *Vallejo Times-Herald,* July 27, 1969, p. 1.

FOP scores Kerner Report. *New York Times,* February 14, 1968, p. 1.

Gallup Poll on police unions. *New York Times,* January 12, 1967, p. 52.

Hollister police back on the beat. *San Francisco Chronicle,* November 17, 1970.

Hopeful sign in strike. *Vallejo News Chronicle,* July 21, 1969, p. 1.

It wasn't easy, but strike's over. *Antioch Daily Ledger,* July 14, 1970, p. 1.

Labor letter. *Wall Street Journal,* November 16, 1968, p. 1.

Labor letter. *Wall Street Journal,* February 18, 1969, p. 1.

Legal action is delayed. *Antioch Daily Ledger,* July 6, 1970, p. 1.

Leon H. Keyserling police salary survey. *New York Times,* March 22, 1960, p. 39.

New punch in police bargaining. *Oakland Tribune,* November 9, 1969, p. 1.

New ruling on police fire strikes. *The Sacramento Union,* December 30, 1970.

Newark FOP challenges overtime rule. *New York Times,* June 6, 1965, p. 74.

Newark police begin strict enforcement of the law. *New York Times,* October 21, 1968, p. 1.

Opinion research study. *New York Times,* December 19, 1968, p. 55.

PBA wins state trooper run-off election. *New York Times,* August 31, 1969, p. 25.

Pennsylvania State Police's pay raise. *San Francisco Chronicle,* December 25, 1970.

Pitt police back Antioch. *Antioch Daily Ledger,* July 13, 1970, p. 1.

Police adopt policies for pay, benefits. *San Diego Evening Tribune,* November 1, 1969.

Police bar strikes in proposed union. *New York Times,* November 3, 1969.

Police, city stalemated; yard worker are "sick." *Antioch Daily Ledger,* July 13, 1970, p. 1.

Police, fire walkout ends. *Vallejo Times-Herald,* July 22, 1969, p. 1.

Police, firemen strike; court injunction ignored. *Vallejo News Chronicle,* July 17, 1969, p. 1.

Police force in Hollister calls strike. *Sacramento Bee,* November 13, 1970.

Police picket city hall. *New York Times,* October 19, 1968, p. 1.

Policemen in state considering unions. *San Diego Evening Tribune,* October 29, 1969.

Public protection will be provided. *Vallejo News Chronicle,* July 18, 1969, p. 1.

Shooting in a copless town. *San Francisco Chronicle,* November 16, 1970.

Two unions slate outdoor meeting for Monday night. *Vallejo Times-Herald,* July 20, 1969, p. 1.

Uniform groups won't report for shifts in morning. *Vallejo Times-Herald,* July 16, 1969, p. 1.

Vallejo to seek court restraining order on walkout, *Vallejo Times-Herald,* July 17, 1969, p. 1.

We'll work 12-hour shifts—Carlson. *Antioch Daily Ledger,* July 9, 1970, p. 1.

Why policemen are unhappy. *New York Times,* October 24, 1968, p. 59.

Wilmington, Delaware police barred from FOP membership, *New York Times,* September 12, 1965, p. 129.

$1,200 more. *Antioch Daily Ledger,* July 14, 1970, p. 1.

OTHER

Reile, A. S.: Why the unionization of police forces is in the public interest, *The Police Yearbook—1958.*

American Federation of Labor, *Proceedings,* 1897.

Chicago City Council, *Proceedings,* January 26, 1913.

New York City Department of Labor, *Report On the Recognition and Organization of Unionized Police, New York City,* 1958.

Hearings, Committee on the District of Columbia, United States Senate, 66th Congress, 1st Session, September 1919.

Municipalities and the Law In Action, (Washington, D.C.: The National Institute of Municipal Law Officers, 1941).

Report of the Commissioner of Police for the City of Boston, 1920.

The American Almanac: The U. S. Book of Facts, Statistics, and Information, 1970, New York, Grosset & Dunlop, 1969.

The Municipal Yearbook 1969, Washington, D. C., International City Management Association, 1969.

The Police Problem in New York City, New York, The Bureau of City Betterment of the Citizens Union of the City of New York, November 1906.

The Police Yearbook of 1970, Washington, D. C., International Association of Chiefs of Police, 1970.

1966 Municipal Yearbook, Washington, D. C., International City Managers Association, 1966.

1966-1969 Annual Salary Survey, Peace Officers Association of California, Inc., October 30, 1968.

1969-1970 Annual Salary Survey, Peace Officers Association of California, Inc., October 28, 1969.

INDEX

187